# The Violet Hour

## ALSO BY KATIE ROIPHE

# THE
# VIOLET
# HOUR

Great Writers at the End

KATIE ROIPHE

virago

VIRAGO

First published in the United States in 2016 by The Dial Press
First published in Great Britain in 2016 by Virago Press

1 3 5 7 9 10 8 6 4 2

Copyright © 2016 by Katie Roiphe

A CIP catalogue record for this book
is available from the British Library.

Hardback ISBN 978-0-349-00852-3
Trade paperback ISBN 978-0-349-00851-6

Printed and bound in Great Britain by
Clays Ltd, St Ives plc

Papers used by Virago are from well-managed forests
and other responsible sources.

MIX
Paper from
responsible sources
FSC® C104740

Virago Press
An imprint of
Little, Brown Book Group
Carmelite House
50 Victoria Embankment
London EC4Y 0DZ

An Hachette UK Company
www.hachette.co.uk

www.virago.co.uk

To Anne Roiphe

# Contents

# The Violet Hour

# Prologue

I forget how to breathe. I am being pulled underwater. The taxi driver carries me into the emergency room because I've passed out in the cab and my mother can't lift a twelve-year-old.

In *How We Die*, Sherwin Nuland describes the physical effects of pneumonia: "The microscopic air sacs called alveoli swell and are destroyed by inflammation. As a result, proper exchange of gases is prevented, and blood oxygen diminishes while carbon dioxide may build up until vital functions can no longer be sustained. When oxygen levels drop below a critical point, the brain manifests it by further cell death."

Someone puts a mask on my face. I taste the sweetness of the oxygen, like tasting sky.

I have a 107-degree fever. At home, my mother had put me in a bathtub with ice cubes in it. In intensive care, there are tubes or snakes in my arms; there are good or evil nurses. An intern sticks a needle into an artery to measure my oxygen levels. In the next bed over, a baby's heart stops.

This is when I start writing this book.

———

Three weeks later I leave the hospital, but I do not get completely better.

The cough is so bad it's like an animal that lives with me and sleeps in my bed. On the worst days my mother tries to get me to stay home from school, but I am adamant about going.

I have fevers every evening, shivering through dinner, homework, bath. There is no question that this is the way I will feel forever; there is no idea of after the fever, or if there is any idea like that, it is wan, unconvincing, because the fever is a world.

I wake up with my nightgown soaked in sweat, the sheets wet with sweat. The sweat is shameful, something to be hidden; the fever is also something shameful.

Doctors are consulted, antibiotics prescribed. I go into the hospital and come out of the hospital. My father, who is a doctor himself, is very quiet when the doctors talk. There is no name for what is wrong with me.

One day when I cough, there is blood in the tissue. I taste blood in my mouth. I know this means that I am dying, and so

I do the sensible thing and tell no one, not my mother, my father, my sisters, my doctor.

I am not exactly a worldly twelve. During my first pneumonia, a friend of my mother's makes me a little cardboard-box house, with a furry toy mouse in a blue gingham dress, with little bedspreads and armchairs and clothes and books; I love this house and play with it, even though I'm too old for it. I am a girl who still plays with a fur mouse in a dress, trying to get a handle on coughing up blood.

My mother plots and pleads and calls up doctor friends to get me an appointment with a famous lung specialist. When I am finally in his office she explains that I can't walk up a flight of stairs in our house without being out of breath. The doctor asks me how I feel. I don't say anything about the blood I am coughing up. I say, "I feel fine."

In the meantime, I am reading strange books. I am reading exclusively books about genocide: Primo Levi, Elie Wiesel, firsthand accounts of the Armenian genocide. I have a great, endless appetite for these books, not just for people dying but people dying in great numbers, including children, wars, massacres, naked bodies in trenches. I read them one after another. I am reading with something like desire. I want to see children die.

My mother buys me silk nightgowns for the hospital, because cotton hospital pajamas with their gaping holes and faded prints and little ties are demoralizing. The big clustering groups of doctors and residents and medical students lift up these frothy honeymoon nightgowns to listen, one after another, to my mysterious lungs. I am embarrassed to be half naked in front of a crowd of young doctors.

A family of Pentecostal Christians comes to visit the diabetic child I am sharing a room with. They light candles, and start chanting in Spanish to banish the devil, and throw rice, which is surprisingly loud as it hits the floor. The nurse comes in and screams at them for lighting candles in the hospital, especially around my oxygen. They blow out the candles, and the minute the nurse leaves, they light them again. They offer to banish the devil over me, and my mother lets them.

I write a story in the school literary magazine about a girl in the hospital, which ends with a voice calling to her: "Come to me, daughter of the wind." The voice is calling her to give in, pack it up; it's almost cellular, this voice, something in the girl's body telling her to stop fighting, to go under. The line brings something back to me now. How death, this thing you are resisting, fighting, terrified of, suddenly turns and becomes seductive. As Virginia Woolf writes in her dazzling meditation "On Being Ill," "illness often takes on the disguise of love, and plays the same odd tricks."

Eventually I have a test where they put a tube down my throat and inject white dye into my lungs. This is supposed to show the doctors whether the chronic infection is localized enough for them to operate. In the X-rays, it looks like there are snow-covered trees in my lungs.

The night before my surgery, the sound of bagpipes floats through the hospital hallways. The sound frightens me, it is so incongruous and beautiful and funereal. My mother explains that the son of a policeman has cancer, and the police have sent a troupe of bagpipe players to play for him.

The operation lasts seven hours. They remove half of one of my lungs. In the recovery room, a tube in my throat, tubes draining my lungs through small holes between my ribs, a tube in my arm, I swim up from the anesthetic and ask for my mother. A nurse says to me, "You are too old to call for your mother."

My older sister is in medical school. She is not intimidated by the tubes and climbs into the bed with me, which cheers me up. She brings me a red tin of madeleines that she has made. My best friend does not visit me in the hospital. She has decided to stop being friends with me.

When I come home, I am sixty pounds. I am too weak to open a door. My hair has fallen out in the front, so I have to cut it all off. My father takes me on slow walks down our street, but I can't yet make it around a city block.

You read about soldiers who have trouble coming back into civilian life. They can't fit themselves back into everyday pre-occupations: whether to wear a winter coat, whether to go to a party, whether to eat lunch. They are totally and completely wrapped up in the shocking time; they are constantly drawn back to it; they are in love with it the way you love someone who has hurt you: It will not let them go. In the end it doesn't matter if they are the best or worst hours of your life; all of that is irrelevant and stripped away: You are drawn back into it. After the hospital, I feel like that, but I don't know what to call it. I go back to *The Road from Home: The Story of an Armenian Girl.*

———

Maurice Sendak sat with the people he loved as they were dying and drew them. To some, this might seem like a perverse or weird thing to do, but I understand it completely and intuitively. In fact, I am doing something like it myself.

I am writing about deaths. Not the deaths of people I loved but of writers and artists who are especially sensitive or attuned to death, who have worked through the problem of death in their art, in their letters, in their love affairs, in their dreams. I've picked people who are madly articulate, who have abundant and extraordinary imaginations or intellectual fierceness, who can put the confrontation with mortality into words—and in one case images—in a way that most of us can't or won't.

It would be hard to pin down why I chose these particular people. I was drawn to each one of them by instinct, felt some heat coming off their writing, some intuition that they could answer or complicate or refine the questions I was asking myself, that their deaths, laid open, would show me what I needed to see. I chose writers who meant something to me, whose voices were already in my head, whose approach toward death was extreme in one direction or another: inspiring or bewildering or heroic or angry. I chose lives that were puzzles, that confused and intrigued and unsettled me, that threw me for a loop. I chose people whose imagination is bigger or greater or holds out some possibility of more intense perception or precision of description than I would be capable of myself. I was thinking: If it's nearly impossible to capture the approach of death in words, who would have the most hope of doing it?

Once I settled on my subjects, I combed through their work, their letters, their journals, their notes, their postcards, their scribbled cartoons, their interviews, their manuscripts, for glimmers of their evolving thoughts and feelings on dying. I talked to sons, daughters, lovers, wives, ex-wives, friends, caretakers, housekeepers, night nurses. I learned how they faced or did not face, embraced or evaded, made peace with or raged against death, sometimes all at once. I wrote down jokes they made in the hospital, or a haircut that cheered them up, or a moment where they took a piece of scrap paper and wrote something under harrowing and improbable circumstances.

Sigmund Freud, in great pain, refused anything stronger than aspirin so he could think clearly, and finally chose the moment of his own death. Susan Sontag, on the other hand, fought her death to the end, believing on some deep irrational level she would be the one exception to mortality. Maurice Sendak worked his whole life on death, taming his fear and obsession through drawings, and finally creating out of his wild imagination a beautiful painterly dream to comfort himself. The month before he died, John Updike laid his head on his typewriter, because it was too hard to type up his final poems about dying and he was ready to give up, and then he found the strength to finish them. Dylan Thomas, in his last days, left his mistress downstairs at a party and went upstairs to sleep with the hostess, hurtling along with his peerless mixture of vitality and self-destruction; as he put it, "I sang in my chains like the sea."

There are in these deaths glimpses of bravery, of beauty, of crushingly pointless suffering, of rampant self-destruction, of truly terrible behavior, of creative bursts, of superb devotion, of glitteringly accurate self-knowledge, and of magnificent delusion. There are things I could never have guessed or theorized or anticipated, and it is in the specifics, the odd, surprising details, the jokes, the offhand comments, that some other greater story is told and communicated.

Why did Sendak want to draw death? Why did Annie Leibovitz take her controversial and startling last photographs of Susan Sontag as she lay dying and after she died? Why did the Victorians photograph dead babies propped up in prams and on people's laps? Why did the Romantics make death masks? "I do it because I can't not do it," as Sendak said about his art generally. "Something malfunctions in me."

I think if I can capture a death on the page, I'll repair or heal something. I'll feel better. It comes down to that.

At first I thought I was trying to understand death, but then I realized that was a lie I was telling myself. I want to see death.

When I say "see," I mean something specific and bookish. Another, bolder journalist might go to a hospice to talk to people who are dying, might fly to war zones, might interview patients in Ebola hospitals, but my way of seeing has always been different, shyer. To see the world I've always opened a book.

———

I start with a room. Freud's room, with its French doors overlooking the blossoming almond tree; John Updike's institutionally homey room at the upscale hospice in Danvers, Massachusetts; Susan Sontag's last room at Sloan Kettering; Dylan Thomas's room at St. Vincent's, with its oxygen tent; Maurice Sendak's sprawling "comfort care" room at Danbury Hospital. I very conspicuously do not belong in these rooms.

This is one of our few powerful taboos. Sherwin Nuland writes, "Modern dying takes place in the modern hospital, where it can be hidden, cleansed of its organic blight, and finally packaged for modern burial. We can now deny the power not only of death but of nature itself." We do not see death the way people in other centuries saw it all the time—a mother in childbirth in a four-poster mahogany bed, a baby carried down the hall in a sheet, a child burning up with scarlet fever. We do not see people die in our homes very often, and death is something that we can forget about, cordon off. But the heat or curiosity is there. Susan Sontag once wrote that "the appetite for pictures showing bodies in pain is as keen, almost, as the desire for ones that show bodies naked." She captures a near-pornographic feel to death, a desire to see that feels illicit, wrong.

I have thought a lot about this desire to see a death. A reporter asked Annie Leibovitz about the photographs she took of people close to her—Susan Sontag, and her father—dying and dead, and she said: "You find yourself reverting to what you know. It's almost like a protection of some kind. You go back into yourself. You don't really know quite what you're doing. I didn't really analyze it. I felt driven to do it."

Is that drive prurient, voyeuristic? Is there something sick or unhinged or vulturish about it?

Even if there is, the curiosity feels natural. For me it involves going back.

———

The work I did for this book included talking to a lot of strangers about their mothers and fathers and husbands and close friends dying. In the beginning, I felt uncomfortable for intruding, for asking them to dredge up a dark, impossible time. I wrote long apologetic letters and emails about how much I understood if they didn't want to talk to me. "I don't want to impose on your privacy," I would write. "I would be very grateful for your time but completely understand if you don't want to talk." The people I was interviewing frequently started reassuring *me*; that was how awkwardly I was coming across. But the conversations we had ended up, very often, being among the most extraordinary I've had in my life.

The story of a death is intimate, scary, huge, but maybe in some ways easier to tell a stranger. Curled up in my bed, I talked on the phone for hours to several people. Some called me back or emailed with new things they remembered or thoughts or bits of analysis. Some stopped and started. Some said they didn't want to talk and then said they would. Some said they didn't want to talk and proceeded to talk for hours. One cried on a barstool. One would only answer my questions while he painted my portrait, so I sat in his studio, trying and mostly failing not to move or gesture, while we talked. Sometimes interviews would turn into teas and lunches and drinks and visits to museums and sprawl out over months. The talk was electric; the desire to explain, to mull over with someone also invested, was undeniable, a surprise. The people I talked to were generous with their impressions, deeply personal reactions, fraught moments, but they also wanted to talk about something that isn't talked about, all of us uneasily circling a taboo.

One of the people I interviewed for the book said to me at one point: "I don't question your motives." I was floored with gratitude because, of course, I was always questioning my own motives: I roiled through them constantly. Why am I doing this? Why do I want to know this? What normal person wants to blunder into this hushed and sacred space? Why do I want to get this close to a death? Why can't I respect the decent boundaries?

At various points in the years I was writing this book I wanted to stop, because it was tricky, dangerous, unwieldy, or confusing, or making me anxious, but I couldn't stop. The material kept calling to me in a way I only partially understood. I felt compelled by these stories, obsessed with them; they were like puzzles or mysteries I couldn't leave alone or stop thinking about.

Ancient Egyptians used to read the *Book of the Dead* to learn practical tips on how to navigate the underworld—like how to not have your head cut off in the underworld, or how to take the form of a crocodile in the underworld, or how to not enter the underworld upside down—but we don't have a *Book of the Dead*.

The problem with the project is that it could have gone on forever. There were so many deaths I wanted to dive into: William Blake's happy death, where he sat up in bed and saw angels; Honoré de Balzac killing himself through work and coffee; Primo Levi's probably suicidal fall down the stairs; Christopher Hitchens's fierce commitment to reporting his death; Virginia Woolf's descent into the river, with stones in her overcoat; Franz Kafka's starving, like his hunger artist, in the sanatorium; Leo Tolstoy leaving his wife and dying near a train station at the stationmaster's house; F. Scott Fitzgerald's heart attack in Hollywood. All of them seemed to call to me.

I don't believe that you can learn how to die, or gain wisdom, or prepare, and the work I have done on this book has, if anything, confirmed that suspicion, but I do think you can look at a death and be less afraid.

As I was working on them, I found the portraits of these deaths hugely and strangely reassuring. The beauty of the life comes spilling out. The power of an inspiring mind working on the problem. Somehow these sketches were freeing, comforting, exhilarating, in part because the people I was writing about lived great, vivid, gloriously productive lives. There is something about the compression of the final moments, the way everything comes rushing in, the intensity, that is beautiful, even though the death is not.

Maurice Sendak owned Keats's death mask, which he kept in a wooden box. He adored it. He liked to stroke its forehead. I saw it and it was very beautiful. Why would anyone want to own a death mask? I asked myself. But I knew. In a way, I was writing death masks.

————

For some reason when I think of my father's death, I keep going back to the part where he falls onto the marble floor of the lobby of his building. He is on his way back from dinner and a concert. My mother says to him, "Should I call an ambulance?" It is like my mother to ask, to defer to him, the doctor. "No," he says. He is irritated—I can imagine this tone—at the implication that he can't take care of himself. He is in the middle of a massive cardiac arrest.

By the time my sister and I arrive at the hospital, he is dead.

He is nearly eighty-two, but his death feels sudden, out of the blue. He walked twenty blocks to work every day; he scheduled patients until seven o'clock at night; he carried suitcases and bags and babies for the women in his life; he was startlingly healthy for a man his age.

But still I have the sense that before the night of his heart attack, death had begun to appear to him privately as a subject. He had, increasingly, moments of retreat, of withdrawal into himself. He would be absent suddenly, in the middle of a dinner or a walk. He was distracted; he was being taken slowly out of life.

In the weeks before my father died, he had, by chance, a thorough cardiological workup. His doctor told him that he had the heart of a man thirty years younger. And yet, at around that same time, in late November, he suddenly decided to sit down and write the names of all the artists of the paintings and drawings he had collected over sixty years. He didn't think my mother and my sisters and I would otherwise know what they were. Why in the sixty years that he had owned and collected those pictures did he choose that particular moment? He did not consciously know he was about to die, but was he operating out of some deeper, almost cellular imperative? Does the body have some foreshadowing, some knowledge of its own decline, before the mind does? Did he somehow know?

In the emergency room at St. Luke's Hospital, a doctor asks if we want to see the body. I do not want to see the body. I am somehow by this time outside, just through the electric door, in the cold air, the lights of the hospital in my eyes, and my older sister, a psychoanalyst, catches up with me. She tells me it is important to see the body, because if you don't see the body there is no body. I am not able to take this in, and so I don't see the body and there is no body.

———

When I come home from the hospital, my two-and-a-half-year-old is awake, sitting bolt upright, waiting for me, in order to express her outrage that I have left in the middle of the night without telling her.

I tell her that my father has died. I tell her what it means.

I hear myself saying the words, "Sometimes when people get old, their bodies stop working."

*"Sometimes?"*

I pause. "Well, always."

It is a brutal thing to say to a two-year-old; it doesn't even sound true.

In the weeks after my father's death, I'm not functioning at a very high level. I am not, for instance, eating. My father was the one who cooked for our family. He baked bread; caught and cooked bass, trout, salmon, bluefish; picked blackberries and made them into jam, pies; cooked giant turkeys and cranberry breads on Thanksgiving; copied out recipes on yellow legal paper in his terrible scrawling handwriting. The morning I came home from the emergency room after a fall, he brought me homemade biscuits, and the day I brought the baby home from the hospital, he brought me servings of boeuf bourguignon and lamb moussaka to put in the freezer; I seem, in this particular crisis, to be waiting for him to bring me something to eat.

The baby, meanwhile, is going ahead full throttle with the questions. I would like someone to give me a pamphlet on "What to Tell the Baby," but nobody has given me that pamphlet. "Did Pompa have Band-Aids when he dived?" the baby asks. "What was on his Band-Aids when he dived?" She wants, of course, to hear that he had furry, consoling creatures on his Band-Aids. I think of how Freud once referred to "the painful riddle of death." A riddle because there remains some question to be answered, some confusion to be cleared up.

When I was a child I had a turtle called Herman. I named the turtle Herman after my father, in that brief blissful period when my father was the only man on earth. And then the turtle died. I don't know when I was aware that it died, but at a certain point I knew with horror that it was dead. I kept feeding it, changing its cage, and pretending that it was not, in fact, dead. There was very little the turtle did or loved or cared about, after all; there was not a huge gap between the turtle dead and the turtle alive. In the end I took the turtle out to a grassy place and set him free. I told everyone that. That I set him free.

My father stopped smoking when everyone else stopped smoking, when it became clear that smoking was terrible for you, but unlike everyone else, he didn't stop. He would sneak out and smoke. I remember the smell of smoke in his hair, the heavy glass ashtrays in his office. He was not the type for secret vices, even small ones, but he kept his smoking secret. This scared me. I had pumped goldfish full of smoke in science class and watched them float to the surface of the water.

If I am honest, I remember that he was often out of breath at the end of his life; I remember the alarming sound of his ragged breathing, after a couple of blocks, the air running out; I remember how upsetting it was, how I didn't allow myself to hear it. So why did he secretly smoke for decades and destroy his lungs, after he knew they were being destroyed? Why did Freud, one of my father's great heroes along with Trollope, continue to smoke against the explicit urging of his physicians? I have a feeling that my father would have smiled if he came across Freud quoting George Bernard Shaw: "Don't try to live forever, you will not succeed."

———

Is there a last conversation I wish I could have had with my father? I did not have a complicated relationship with him; there were no tangled conflicts to resolve; he knew how much I loved him. What was there to say? But there is something. When he died he was worried about my marriage. He had seen things that made him think my husband would not be around for me and my daughter in the ways he would have hoped. I wish I had told him that I was in the middle of leaving. He would have been relieved. He would have stopped worrying. Why does this matter, as dirt is falling on a coffin? It does though. It matters.

I found in the research for this book that while nearly everyone has a fantasy of a "last conversation," very few people actually have it. It is the fantasy of resolution, of a final cathartic communication that rarely materializes, because the prickliness or reserve or anger that was there all along is still there, because the urgency of death does not clarify muddiness, or lift obstacles, or defuse conflicts, or force us to talk about what matters, however much we wish it would.

Mostly, the last conversation doesn't exist or exists only in parody, in its refusal of meaning, in its Beckett-like embrace of the absurd. Take Philip Roth's mother's last words, "I do not want this soup." We are, most of the time, left with this wild irresolution, this lack of an ending, which may be part of our investment in this mythical conversation, as if things ever end and are not simply cut off.

———

I would not have bought the *New York Post* with the dead baby on the cover, but since it is lying on the table at the coffee shop,

I am reading the story and continuing on page four. The family had driven in from New Jersey. The father was taking a picture on the promenade outside the sea lion exhibit at the Central Park Zoo, and the mother was holding their six-month-old, Gianna, when a branch fell and killed the baby. When I come to the end of the story I feel like I haven't gotten enough detail, but what other detail was I looking for? What more detail could I possibly need?

I had taken my own baby to the Central Park Zoo a few weeks before. I had shown him that giant cuckoo clock with animals and their instruments, the same clock I used to see as a child, on the promenade outside the sea lion exhibit. There is an incantatory quality to reading the *Post* article. Am I telling myself that in a world full of rotting branches on glorious days, my own baby is safely sleeping in a green-painted crib on the bottom floor of my house? Am I trying to prove that this specific tragedy happened to this specific baby and in fact has nothing at all to do with anything that could in any way happen to my baby? As Freud put it, "Our habit is to lay stress on the fortuitous causation of the death—accident, disease, infection, advanced age; in this way we betray an effort to reduce death from a necessity to a chance event."

There is, of course, in all of this fascination with death, with extremities, a primitive, ritualistic dividing of the well from the sick, the alive from the dead, the lucky from the unlucky. Susan Sontag wrote about visiting the very sick in a draft for a short story: "making time to drop by the hospital every day,

is a way of our trying to put ourselves more firmly + irrevoca-
bly in the situation of the well, those who aren't sick, who
aren't going to get sick, as if what happened to him couldn't
happen to one of us."

———

What was my father thinking in those last weeks, when he
seemed so far in retreat? Were those minutes of detachment at
a family meal, that not-there-ness he was increasingly project-
ing, a divesting of interest, a stepping back from life, a renunciation of what he loved, as he intuited it being taken away? I
will never know, and I never talked to him about it. All I can do
is substitute and approximate, extrapolate, fill in the blanks. I
can find out what other people felt. I can comb through other
people's letters and journals and postcards and scribbled notes
in air-conditioned libraries. I can have long coffees with other
people's friends and children.

In *Rabbit at Rest*, John Updike's Rabbit Angstrom has a heart
attack on a sailboat with his granddaughter: "His chest feels
full, his head dizzy, his pulse rustles in his ears, the soaked
space between his shoulder blades holds a jagged pain." And:
"The sense of doom hovering over him these past days has
condensed into reality, as clouds condense into needed rain.
There is a lightness, a lightening, that comes along with misery: vast portions of your life are shorn off, suddenly ignor-
able. You become simply a piece of physical luggage to be
delivered into the hands of others."

How does it feel to come so close to death you can breathe its atmosphere? I can't get back to the year I knew, but I want to come as close as I can.

Before being diagnosed with esophageal cancer, healthy but maybe a little worse for the wear, Christopher Hitchens wrote in his memoir: "I want to stare death in the eye." And it is that staring that is rarely granted to us. Susan Sontag once wrote, "One can't look steadily at death any more than one can stare at the sun." And Freud argues that we can't even imagine our deaths: "It is indeed impossible to imagine our own death; and whenever we attempt to do so we can perceive that we are in fact still present as spectators." And when people we love die, we are so steeped in loss and love and dread that we can't see, much less stare.

It's interesting how quickly the imagination turns death into something else; how quickly, cleverly, resourcefully we flee. "Full fathom five thy father lies . . . Those are pearls that were his eyes." We can, if we work hard enough, make death into pearls. What would it be like if the line were: "Those aren't pearls that were his eyes"?

But how to look if not to stare? In my head I think of what I am doing as biography backward, a whole life unfurling from a death.

I've tried in this book to avoid romanticizing, to look very closely at what is happening without veering off into consolations or euphemisms or evasions or neat conclusions. I have tried to avoid any impulse toward the lyrical, the not quite honest, the falsely redemptive. I wanted to look at what was happening very calmly and clearly.

Secretly, of course, reading through these deaths, what one wants to learn is how to avoid dying altogether. That's the little bit of news one is looking for. Barring that, though, think of Leopold Bloom's fantasy of seducing a woman in a grave-yard in *Ulysses:* "Love among the tombstones. Romeo. Spice of pleasure. In the midst of death we are in life."

Susan Sontag

## DECEMBER 2004

If there is anyone on earth who could decide not to die it would be Susan Sontag; her will is that ferocious, that unbending, that unwilling to accept the average fates or outcomes the rest of us are bound by. She is not someone to be pushed around or unduly influenced by the idea that everyone has to do something or go through something, because she is and always has been someone who rises above. Nonetheless, right before Christmas, she is lying in a bed in Memorial Sloan Kettering Cancer Center, on the Upper East Side of Manhattan, doing something that very much appears to those around her to be dying.

One night she and her friend Sharon DeLano stay up late listening to Beethoven's late string quartets in her hospital room. Sontag is very doped up. She is in a good enough mood to tell Sharon one of her favorite jokes. "Where does the general keep his armies?" Sharon answers, "I don't know." "In his sleevies," Sontag says, smiling.

The next day she is much more sober. When Sharon arrives, Susan is reading the German filmmaker Rainer Werner Fassbinder's juvenilia and they watch two movies together. Sharon has to press pause frequently, because Susan is talking through the whole movie, adding commentary and glosses.

Susan has known Sharon DeLano for a long time. They met in the mid-seventies when Sharon was working as an editor at *The New York Review of Books*. When Susan, who was recovering from her first cancer, doesn't want to be alone, she calls Sharon, who comes up and keeps her company at her Riverside Drive apartment.

Sharon has been an editor at *Vanity Fair*, Random House, and *The New Yorker*, where she edits Susan's work. On the surface, Sharon can seem tough, but to her friends she is warm and funny and ferociously loyal.

Sontag's third cancer comes into focus when Sookhee Chinkhan, her housekeeper, who's been with her for over a decade, sees bruises on her back when she is drawing her bath. Sookhee works for Susan five days a week, cleaning, cooking; there is a running chatter between them that other people are bewildered by.

The diagnosis of myelodysplastic syndrome, which leads to a particularly virulent strain of blood cancer, comes in March 2004. Sontag's son, David Rieff, a journalist in his early fifties, accompanies her to the doctor for a follow-up visit after the initial tests.

David is tall and elegant. He is handsome in the way of a Roman coin. He has the slight air of being crown prince to a country that has suddenly and inexplicably gone democratic.

The doctor lays out the grimmest possible scenario: There is absolutely no chance of remission or cure. He suggests that Sontag do nothing and take the remaining six months or so left to live her life.

In the weeks after Susan is diagnosed, Sookhee notices that sometimes she says, "Wow wow," and closes her eyes. Susan tells her it's the pain.

Inevitably, this latest illness brings back Sontag's first, dire cancer diagnosis in 1975. She was in her early forties when she discovered that she had stage 4 breast cancer. None of the doctors she initially consulted thought she had any hope at all, but she sought out aggressive treatments and she survived. From that point onward, the transcendence of ordinary illness and ordinary endings became incorporated and entangled with who she was—the person who seeks treatment, who solves her disease like a math problem, like a logical puzzle of the highest order. "I am gleaming with survivorship," she wrote in the eighties. The brush with death was incorporated into her dark glamour, her writer's pose. In an essay on photography, she wrote about "the sex appeal of death," and this was a sex appeal that she took on, the danger and thrill of coming near to it, of breathing it in, and turning back.

The extremity of her breast cancer, once she recovered, fed into her long-standing idea of herself as exceptional. Another way to look at this is that her long-standing idea of herself as exceptional fed into the way she handled her cancer. Sharon DeLano says, "Because she was so fierce, because she was confrontational in terms of authority, her instinct was to confront it. She immediately decided that the doctors were wrong. This was a period when the idea of a second opinion was not a very common one . . . and she was so fierce that she went out and got one, and she survived. I think it was a vindication of who she was and how she thought. Because she didn't do the conventional thing, and she thought for herself and she lived. And it sort of reinforced all the things she was and the kind of. thinker that she was. What that meant was that the next time she got sick and the next time, she thought she could do the same thing." Indeed, when she was diagnosed with uterine cancer in 1998, she avidly pursued arduous and aggressive treatments, chemotherapy, surgery, and she survived.

In her notebooks you can see the work of self-mythologizing all along, the labor of it, the relentless taking of raw life materials and shaping them into an idea of herself as exceptional. Everyone does this, of course, but Sontag does it with a million times more commitment, more intensity, and more success than other people. Her myth is all-encompassing, seductive. One of her friends comments that she has "star quality," and he is referring not to her beauty but to her drive for attention, her self-conscious deployment of myth. She berates herself in her journals: "Don't smile so much." "Weakness is a contagion. Strong people rightly shun the weak." It is her will to become that is most spectacular, her constant working on herself, tinkering with it as if it were an essay. She writes at twenty-four, "In the journal I do not just express myself more openly than I could do to any person; I create myself."

Her drive for transformation was always powerful. She went to Berkeley at sixteen, transferring after a semester to the more academically rigorous University of Chicago. There she met a much older professor, Philip Rieff, and after ten days decided to marry him. She got a master's degree in philosophy at Harvard, and then she left Rieff and their four-year-old son, David, for a couple of years to go and study at Oxford and the Sorbonne, when that was what she felt she needed to do.

From girlhood, Sontag's private mythology was predicated on a contempt for the ordinary and a distance from it. She once mocked her good friend Stephen Koch for having a savings account and health insurance, because that was what ordinary, middle-class people had. Intellectuals and artists didn't have savings accounts or health insurance.

In early interviews after her recovery from breast cancer, she seemed intoxicated by her proximity to death. She said the following in an almost giddy interview in *The New York Times* in 1978: "It has added a fierce intensity to my life, and that's been pleasurable. . . . It's fantastic knowing you're going to die; it really makes having priorities and trying to follow them very real to you. That has somewhat receded now; more than two years have gone by, and I don't feel the same sort of urgency. In a way I'm sorry; I would like to keep some of that feeling of crisis. . . . I think it's good to be in contact with life and death. Many people spend their lives defending themselves against the notion that life is melodrama. I think it's good not to damp down these conflicts. . . . You get terrific energy from facing them in an active and conscious way. For me, writing is a way of paying as much attention as possible."

While she was being treated for her breast cancer, she did not stop working or thinking, or struggling to work and think. In the midst of chemotherapy, she was taking notes for her elegant and influential polemic *Illness as Metaphor*. In it she argues against the various fantasies that surround disease. Instead of poetry and emotionally charged beliefs, she argues, patients need clarity, rational thought, and medical information, to prepare themselves for the hard work of the cure. In her hospital room, she wrote in her journal, "I have become afraid of my own imagination," and it was this fear she so brilliantly investigated and rejected in *Illness as Metaphor*. She writes that the imagination, the romantic overlay we give disease, is itself violent, destructive.

———

After the diagnosis of myelodysplastic syndrome, Sookhee sometimes sleeps over in the living room, because Susan does not want to be alone. One night she wakes up to Susan screaming. She is panicked. Sookhee has never seen her like this before. Sookhee sits on the bed and holds her and begins to pray, because that is all that she can think to do. "Please Lord, give Susan peace."

In "The Way We Live Now," her excellent short story about illness, about what it is like to be sick, Sontag writes: "Dying is an amazing high he said to Quentin. Sometimes I feel *so* fucking well, so powerful, it's as if I could jump out of my skin. Am I going crazy, or what? Is it all this attention and coddling I'm getting from everybody, like a child's dream of being loved? Is it the drugs? Or what? I know it sounds crazy but sometimes I think it is a *fantastic* experience." She writes this in 1986 as someone who knows what dying feels like. She writes this as someone who was dying and then turned back.

That spring of 2004, after her diagnosis with leukemia, she turns her apartment into a center for medical research. Everyone is doing Internet searches, and friends are calling with suggestions and doctors' names and obscure studies. Susan's young assistant, Anne Jump, helps her find as much information about the illness as she can. They have gone into crisis mode, and everything is about finding a cure. Susan becomes a student of her disease; she studies, underlining in the leukemia pamphlet. Once, years earlier, she jotted down in her notebooks an Auden quote: "I must have knowledge and a great deal of it before I feel anything."

The night before her first exploratory surgery for breast cancer in 1975, she sat in her hospital room at Sloan Kettering with a close friend. Susan was very much herself, which is to say that she had snapped at the intake nurse who called her "Sue" and brought another well-meaning friend who had tried to talk in the platitudes of adversity almost to tears. And yet all of this snappishness was energy, high spirits of a kind, the imposition of herself on the world.

The sun was going down and she suddenly decided she wanted to write the introduction to Peter Hujar's book of photographs, *Portraits in Life and Death*, which she had agreed to do a long time before but had procrastinated. The portraits of prominent downtown figures included one staggeringly beautiful one of her, lying on a bed, staring upward, in a gray cable sweater; there were also the remarkable photographs of human remains from the catacombs in Palermo from the early sixties.

Hujar had brought the photographs of the catacombs over to Sontag's house on Washington Place after he took them. There was some discussion of coming after Sontag's eleven-year-old son, David, was asleep, so that the photographs wouldn't alarm him and give him nightmares. There were skeletons of children draped in ruffles, skulls with bits of ribbon, skulls with wreaths of flowers; it is not the bones but the remnants of the lives, these little bits of cloth and ribbon, that are terrifying, evocative, that reach out and draw the viewer into the idea that everyone they love will die too.

That evening in the hospital in 1975, her friend found something wide and flat for her to write on, and she scribbled away. The mood of the essay is dreamier than usual. In her hospital bed, she took a romantic, intimate view of death with its "sweet poetry and its panic." Her scrawled sentences have a mesmerized quality too. She was staring at something in the middle distance that we cannot normally see. "We no longer study the art of dying, a regular discipline and hygiene in older cultures," she wrote, "but all eyes, at rest, contain that knowledge."

There was peace in the room as she was writing. To be finishing, to be working: This was important to her. The friend who sat with her leafed through a magazine as the orange dusk flooded the room. The essay, one of her more graceful, unbelabored pieces of writing, took her less than an hour.

Her friend remembers her quoting Samuel Johnson with amusement: "Depend upon it, sir, when a man knows he is to be hanged in a fortnight it concentrates his mind wonderfully." Peals of laughter after saying it.

If Sontag was fierce in her determination to fight in that first experience with cancer, her companion of the time, Nicole Stéphane, was equally fierce. Nicole tracked down Dr. Lucien Israel, who pioneered Sontag's experimental treatment, in Paris. He wrote to Sontag, "I do not think your case is hopeless," and that very faint expression of optimism was enough to spur her on. After the operation for her breast cancer, a radical mastectomy called a Halsted, someone sent flowers to Susan's apartment on Riverside Drive. Nicole threw them off the terrace in rage. Flowers were for death.

Later, in Sontag's private mythology, this fierceness is processed as a by-product of her intellect and determination: her refusal to accept her diagnosis or her mortality, her ability to shake off the metaphors of her illness and *act*. But now, in 2004, with this latest, dire diagnosis, she is laboring to maintain her belief in this specialness; she is now having to work to prop it up. She says to several people, including David, "I don't feel special this time," or "I don't feel lucky this time." She is working to fight off the dread, to find her way back to the luck, the specialness, again.

In the meantime, she doesn't want to be alone. She doesn't like the lights off. She has people coming through all the time, people in attendance. These people offer reassurance that she is who she was. One gets the sense that it is only in the dark, and alone, that she is dying.

———

Her long relationship with Annie Leibovitz, whom Sharon had introduced her to, is by now distant and troubled, but Annie is still in her life. Even at the high point of their relationship, they don't like the label "couple" and prefer "friends" or "lovers." Annie has taken photographs of Susan in hotels, in beds, in baths, that are playful, soft, open, evoking a happier time—unlike the usual daunting photographs of Sontag. They keep separate apartments that overlook each other, in the Chelsea building London Terrace.

That spring she continues to try to go to theaters and restaurants and other public places for a few weeks, but soon has to enter the hospital. As she is packing up for Sloan Kettering, Susan says to Sookhee, "Do you think I am ever going to see this apartment again?" Sookhee says she will. Then Susan says, "When I come back, you have to have a drink with me to celebrate. You have to have a glass of wine." She knows that Sookhee's religion doesn't allow her to drink alcohol; but Sookhee says, "I am sure going to have a glass of wine with you, Susan. I am sure going to have a glass of wine with you."

David is torn about what to say to her. "If I am being honest," he would later write in *The Guardian,* "I cannot say that I ever really thought my mother had much chance of making it. . . . I did keep wondering whether, given the fact that her chances were so poor and she was going to suffer so much, perhaps I should be candid with her. But she so plainly did not want to hear this that I never really came close to doing so."

In Sloan Kettering, Susan undergoes a form of chemotherapy called 5-AZ; the rationale behind it isn't that she will be cured but that it may buy her a little more time. In the meantime, she prepares for a bone marrow transplant under the auspices of the highly regarded Fred Hutchinson Cancer Research Center in Seattle, which holds out the only possibility, however remote, of a total cure. For a woman in her early seventies, this seems an implausible step, but her influential doctors help arrange it. It may be that the influential doctors want to be the doctors who save Susan Sontag, or it may be that they too are drawn in by the magnetic force field of her immense desire to live. Part of her power in the world is that she can break rules and bend expectations, create possibilities where they don't normally exist; she can arrange for an extreme treatment that most people of her age would not normally qualify for, or could not afford. But Sontag expects the world to work for her, and the world does work for her. Gates open for her; the doors to beautiful hotel rooms that she doesn't pay for open for her.

In June, before she leaves for Seattle, she makes a will. She doesn't want to make a will. In fact, she is furious about making a will. There had been a flurry of discussion among her intimates about the fact that she needs to make a will before the transplant. It's possible that she doesn't want to make a will for the same reason Picasso didn't want to make a will: because to make a will means admitting that you are going to die. Sontag is planning to leave the literary estate, the apartment, everything, to David, but she still needs to make an official will. Finally, over Susan's protests, her friends send an estate lawyer to the hospital room at Sloan Kettering. And Susan is angry at everyone around her, who all seem to be colluding in the question of the will. She makes the will, but she is enraged the whole time.

Sontag never wrote directly about her experience of illness. David calls *Illness as Metaphor* "anti-autobiographical," and that is exactly what it is, in its studied resistance to confession, its superb channeling of the heat of personal experience into pure intellectual contemplation. In the introduction to that book, she announces that she is *not* going to write about "what it is really like to emigrate to the kingdom of the ill and live there." She says elsewhere in the book that she didn't think it would be useful "to tell yet one more story in the first person of how someone learned that she or he had cancer, wept,

38

struggled, was comforted, suffered, took courage . . ." When her French publisher wanted to put her photograph on the cover of their edition of *Illness as Metaphor*, she objected strongly.

At the time she is diagnosed with her last cancer, she is under contract to write a memoir about her earlier illnesses. She isn't, however, writing that book. She's writing another book instead: a novel about Japan, with different time periods spliced together, with the word "Karaoke" in the title.

———

"She arrived at the hospital believing that she had prepared herself for the procedure," wrote her friend the writer and physician Jerome Groopman, in his 1998 *New Yorker* piece about bone marrow transplants in Seattle. "She would soon learn what I had learned: that it is not a procedure for which anyone can be prepared."

Sontag reads this piece, with its graphic descriptions of the suffering that awaits her, while doing her voracious research of the medical options in New York. Sharon emailed it to her from the *New Yorker* archives.

On June 9, Annie flies with Susan to Seattle in a private plane. In the weeks leading up to the transplant, while Susan prepares for the procedure, her friend Juliane Lorenz, a German film editor and Rainer Werner Fassbinder's last companion, stays with her in a two-bedroom suite with a kitchen at the

Marriott next to the Fred Hutchinson Center. Susan is feeling relatively well and is almost a tourist. With Sharon, she visits the new library, which was designed by Rem Koolhaas. She takes ferry rides.

A roster of caretakers fly out to stay with her. Annie's office and Susan's assistant, Anne Jump, coordinate a schedule so that Susan will never be alone. Most of these caretakers are people who have worked for Susan at one time—Karla Eoff, Ben Yeoman, Peter Perrone, and Sookhee. The others— Sontag's close friend and Italian translator Paolo Dilonardo, Sharon and David and Annie—fly in when they can. Sharon leaves *The New Yorker* in September and begins coming out for longer chunks of time.

Susan liked having someone familiar with her at all times. She was demanding, difficult, charming. Her caretakers would stay with her twelve or sixteen hours a day. "Once you were there, she was like glue," Peter Perrone says.

Peter radiates the paradoxical serenity of the perpetual seeker. He is small, bald, gentle, somehow evoking saffron-clad monks drifting through ancient carved temples in Cambodia. He had spent time doing hospice work. He first met Susan in the eighties when he began doing research for her. He is one of the many people who occupied an ambiguous middle ground between friend and employee, who moved from working for her to being an intimate, who were devoted to her with a kind of passion and absoluteness most people are unable to elicit or uninterested in eliciting from those whom they pay for various kinds of help.

When Peter arrived in Seattle in July, Sontag was preparing for the treatment. One night they went out for Japanese food—without eating anything raw, which could cause a dangerous infection in someone whose immune system was so compromised—and then they saw *Spider-Man 2*. They sat nestled amidst the teenagers on dates. She particularly liked the flying sequence. Peter thought, if illness *does* have to have metaphors, a superhero soaring above a city would not be a bad one.

Somewhere in this same time period, Peter remembers, she had a moment of doubt: Should she go through with the transplant now that she was feeling a little better from the chemo? They were sitting across from each other in a restaurant, holding chopsticks, like they had sat in restaurants in New York. He remembers this doubt as a flicker, a passing thought she confessed to him then dismissed. She would never give up the hope of a cure, and he knew she would never give up hope of the cure, but it was there for a moment between them: the possibility that she could. That she could walk away from the transplant and take what little bit of life was left to her.

Several years before she was diagnosed with her first breast cancer, Sontag wrote in her notebooks: "All my life I have been thinking about death, + it is a subject I am now getting a little

tired of. Not, I think, because I am closer to my own death—
but because death has finally become real (>Death of Susan)."
Susan is Susan Taubes.

Susan Taubes was needy, doomed, depressive, elegant. The
two Susans had met on the steps of Widener Library at Harvard when Sontag was in graduate school. Sontag may or may
not have had an affair with the other Susan's husband. When
Susan Taubes drowned herself while vacationing in the Hamp-
tons, Sontag was called to identify the body, because her name
was found on a note in Taubes's wallet. She drove out with her
friend Stephen Koch, and together they went into the morgue.
The officer pushed a button and a vinyl curtain lifted. The
body was covered, from the neck down, in paper printed with
"Suffolk County New York." The officer said, "Is this your
friend?" Susan looked. "It certainly is." Afterward, her hand
was shaking too much to sign the paperwork. When they
walked out to the car, she said to Koch, "She finally did it, the
stupid woman."

Her frustration with Susan Taubes was that of someone who
can't understand how anyone wouldn't cling to life in any form
at any cost. As she told her doctor, Stephen Nimer, she didn't
care about "quality of life": She cared about life, and it was this
absolute value that would be tested in Seattle.

For a few days in July, Sontag has to be isolated in a radiation
room and radiated. Jerome Groopman explains that in this extreme and harrowing treatment, the stem cell transplant re-
cipient is essentially "brought as close to death as is clinically

sustainable." He continues, "It is a treatment of last resort. Even when all goes well, it represents an experience beyond our ordinary imaginings—the ordeal of chemotherapy taken to a near-lethal extreme." The patient is put in isolation for a few days because of the intensity and toxicity of the radiation. Anne Jump sent her a copy of *Don Quixote*, which she takes into the room while she is radiated.

When she was still healthy, at sixty-nine, Sontag sold her archive to UCLA, but she was very adamantly not winding up. She commented at the time: "Selling the archive is not, 'Now it's all over, and I'm packing up and getting ready to think about my estate.' I don't feel this is one of the gestures that one performs toward the end of one's life." Note the flagrant irrationality of this comment: One doesn't sell one's papers at twenty-five; in fact, selling one's papers is precisely one of those gestures that one performs toward the end of one's life. But the idea of even being "toward" the end of her life was impossible for Sontag, on the verge of seventy, to accept or process or utter on the record in an interview.

One transplant patient whose skin was badly burned by the especially harsh radiation said, "I looked like a lobster and thought I had bugs crawling on me." Sontag undergoes a slightly less extreme version of the radiation, but the effects of the treatment are unimaginable nonetheless. With a severely compromised immune system, the patient is afterward susceptible to all kinds of opportunistic fungus, sores, infections, even in the most successful version of the treatment, the body is broken down, destroyed in order to be rebuilt.

Annie would say later: "She was so brave. It was amazing. It was too much." And those words would appear to crystallize the reaction of many of those around her: *It was too much.*

Sontag wrote in her journals in May of 1976: "I'm mortified by being ill—this illness anyway. But I'm also enthralled by it. Sickness is a form of being 'interesting.' Yet I'm also repelled by it. The vulgarity, the <u>indiscretion</u> of being ill! It makes me want to shut up. My body is talking louder, more plainly than I ever could."

For a while Sontag doesn't want to watch movies in her hospital room in Seattle. She refuses the weighty foreign films that she normally likes, which Anne Jump had packed up and sent out from her apartment. There's much talk in the inner circle about how to get her to watch them, since it seems a good way to keep her entertained during the long hospital hours. Finally Sharon brings her some American musicals, and then suddenly she wants to watch movies: Cary Grant, Fred Astaire, *The African Queen, Kiss Me Kate, Singing in the Rain, It Happened One Night, Funny Face, The Philadelphia Story, Some Like It Hot, To Have and Have Not, Casablanca,* often two movies in a night.

In her notebooks, Sontag claims that Susan Taubes's suicide is important to her because it makes death "real." Did it, though? Susan Taubes's suicide certainly remained with Sontag for a long time; it haunts the journals, hovering in the margins as a problem to be solved; she seems to be scribbling around it, fiddling with it. In 1970, she writes in her notebooks: "An essay to write—on death. The two deaths in my life.

"1938: Daddy: far away, unassimilable.

"1969: Susan: same name as me; ma sosie ['my double'], also unassimilable."

Eventually she wrote a story based on Taubes's suicide, called "Debriefing," which contains the following passage: "Some nights, I dream of dragging Julia back by her long hair, just as she's about to jump into the river. Or I dream she's already in the river: I am standing on my roof, facing New Jersey; I look down and see her floating by, and I leap from the roof, half falling, half swooping like a bird, and seize her by the hair and pull her out." She replays the moment of her friend's death: pause, rewind, play. Here again is the recurring fantasy of cheating death, the last-minute reprieve, the swooping bird that carries you back to safety. This image of dragging her friend back by the hair is so vivid, so startling, and yet it is a dream. You can't drag someone who is dying back by the hair.

———

In August, Sontag goes in for the bone marrow transplant. For a while afterward it is hard to tell if it's working; even in the best-case scenario, transplant patients are very badly off after their procedure, before the body remakes itself. In Sontag's case, the medical information is hard to parse; the team announces that the graft is going well, but then there are complications, setbacks, signs to read and interpret, signals from blood work and biopsies. She certainly doesn't seem, to those who are with her, to be doing too well.

When Peter arrives to take care of her again in the middle of October, he bursts into tears when he sees her, because she is so changed from when he was out in July, before the transplant. Her face and body are blown up from the steroids, her skin stenciled with sores and lesions.

Annie will take pictures of her looking much like this. Her hair is white, cropped like a man's. There are tubes running down her chest, a catheter tube snaking down the sheets. Her stomach is swollen like a pregnant woman's, and her hospital-issue pajamas slip up to reveal a leg mottled with sores, a leg that could belong to someone who is a thousand years old. But what is most shocking is that the familiar, iconic face, the face of the photographs, has vanished. The fierceness in her eyes, the drama of her features, is replaced by a new puffiness, a new indistinctness, as if she is blurred, as if she has transmogrified into an ordinary person, exactly the kind of ordinary person she swore to herself she would never become.

There is the same intimacy as in those other photographs Annie has taken of her in various beds, the ones in far-flung hotels—the Gritti Palace in Venice, Grand Hotel Quisisana in Capri—that are playful, that hint, more than hint, of nights spent together, but here there is no play, just the intimacy, this time doleful or cold, it's hard to tell. Annie does not analyze why she takes these pictures, but she takes them. David will hate these pictures—he calls them "carnival images of celebrity death." Anne Jump will never bring herself to look at them.

Susan had written, "Photography also converts the whole world into a cemetery. Photographers, connoisseurs of beauty, are also—wittingly or unwittingly—the recording angels of death." And she wrote, "The appetite for pictures showing bodies in pain is as keen, almost, as the desire for ones that show bodies naked." Still, Annie seems fairly sure that Susan wouldn't have minded the pictures. She writes in the introduction to *A Photographer's Life:* "Perhaps the pictures completed the work she and I had begun together when she was sick in 1998." She does not put it this way, but the photographs may have been Annie's way of fighting illness as metaphor, her own visual person's equivalent of Susan's brilliant argument; she may have wanted to counteract the fantasies, the embellishments, the imaginative veil we usually throw over sickness, with the way it truly looked.

In one difficult patch, Sookhee comes to visit for a week. Susan finds it comforting to have her there, chattering like she used to in Susan's living room at London Terrace. Susan mentions the twins that Annie is having through a surrogate mother. She had been there for Annie's pregnancy and the birth of her first daughter, Sarah Cameron Leibovitz, three years earlier. Annie is, in her own way, busy thwarting mortality with all of this reproducing in her fifties. Annie had not told Susan about the twins right away, presumably to protect her a little from the onward march of life, but when she finally did, Susan was pleased. "Do you know they are going to name one of them Susan?" she asks Sookhee. "I know," Sookhee says. "We are going to have a Susan with us all the time."

Often, when he is not traveling, David flies in. It is a vast understatement to say that his personal style is formal rather than expressive. He writes later in his memoir, "Perhaps some people transcend themselves when a loved one becomes ill, become demonstrative where before they were inhibited or withholding, and cheerful where before they were morose. But even if that's the case, I was not able to become one of them." His way of helping, of entering the situation, is to talk to the doctors. He gives his mother confidence in the treatment. He renews her sense of intelligent, rational, informed people being on her side in the fight against the cancer. She does not expect him to be one of the caretakers, one of the people attending intimately to her physical needs, and he is not.

David has his own doubts about her continuing treatment, but he sees his role as upholding her belief in her survival. He describes what he was doing as "concocting lawyer's brief after Jesuitical argument in support of what my mother so plainly wanted to hear. Cheerleading her to her grave was the way I sometimes thought of it." He does not doubt that she wants to continue her treatment, though he doubts whether continuing treatment is the right thing to do, and then he doubts his own doubts. But now he is buoying her when the difficulty, or the hopelessness, of the treatments threatens to overtake her. As he later wrote, "my task had to be to help her as best as I could to go on believing that she would survive." Also: "Never for a moment, during the course of my mother's illness, did I think she could have 'heard' that she was dying."

In the room, they put up a piece of paper on the wall where she can watch the number of days that have gone by since the transplant. These fresh white pieces of paper offer a seductive visual: "day 1," "day 2," "day 3." These days mark her new life, her new body, her new beginning. The idea is that on day 100, if the transplant has worked, she might be able to go back to New York.

However, the optimism of the calendar is not carried into the room. The news from the doctors is not promising, and the suffering is breathtaking.

David was amazed by his mother's continuing faith in medicine and by her ability to beat the odds. At the worst moments, he thought to himself, She really does not know what is happening to her; she still believes that she is going to survive. It was part of his role, as he saw it, to mirror this belief back to her as best he could. "The truth is that I was afraid to feel anything, not least because I was so acutely aware of what my mother wanted from me—to believe that she would once more overcome the odds and recover from her disease."

How is it possible not to accept that you are dying if everyone around you knows it and if your body itself is making that argument in as vivid and convincing a way as possible? There is of course the natural clouding of the mind that comes with the drugs, with the pain, with the anxiety, with the sheer psychological strain of being laid out on a hospital bed for four months at a stretch, but there is, perhaps, more to it than that. David pointed out that his mother's belief in her exceptional status, in her will, could have muddied her understanding, that on some deep level she didn't believe that she would face extinction. Even if you know in a rational sense that you are mortal, you can still allow yourself to think: Not this time. You can evade the absoluteness of the death, with the idea that you might have two or ten or thirty years left, with the idea that you are not going to die of this particular illness. After all, it is entirely possible to be forty-five and feel like you are twenty-five, to have no innate connection with your chronological age, no intrinsic physical grasp of it; surely it is possible to be dying and feel like you are not dying, not yet.

Sontag was also a person who took creative liberties with the truth. Which is to say that she lied. Many of her lies were typical ones. She lied about quitting smoking; she lied about lovers; she lied to friends about other friends. But mostly she lied to protect the mythology she had constructed for herself. If she had to choose between the literal truth and her mythology, she would choose her mythology. This led her to strange, inconsequential lies; she would lie, for instance, about the price of her apartment on Riverside Drive, because she wanted to seem like she was an intellectual who drifted into a lovely apartment and did not spend a lot of money on real estate, like a more bourgeois, ordinary person. This sort of lie is interesting because it is in the service of image, of the creation of self that she was always mindful of; she would bend the outside world, in other words, to the powerful inner picture she had of her life. Not everyone does this. Not everyone can do this. And one imagines here the greatest lie, that she was recovering, and the greatest myth she had engineered to date, that of the survivor, of the incandescent defeat of death itself. When someone lies to protect and further their mythology, do they also lie to themselves?

As he watched his mother decline, David struggled with the dissonance between her intellectual position on illness—which argued for logic, rationality, science, clear-sightedness—and the murky reality of the hospital room. The purity and charisma of the ideas Sontag laid out in *Illness as Metaphor* are irresistible, and yet this time around, for Sontag, seeing clearly and absorbing information would have led only to the certain knowledge that she would die. In this final confrontation with cancer, she needed instead consolation; she needed fantasy; she needed *not* to think clearly. In the end, Sontag couldn't live her illness without metaphor; she needed the idea of a fight even after the fight was lost. It's interesting to see the scratched-out lines of the notebook entries. In the middle of her first illness, she wrote: "I feel like the Vietnam War. My illness is invasive, colonizing. They're using chemical warfare on me." She scratched it out because she was determined *not* to think this way about illness, because that was the intellectual position she staked out for herself—*not* to romanticize. And yet here it is, under the pen marks, the natural tendency to think in battles, in war, the irresistible instinct to be a warrior.

———

The hospital masseuse's mother comes in and gives Susan a haircut, which pleases her. She can't lift her head far off the pillow, so this haircut requires unusual skill and dexterity with the scissors. But a haircut matters, even on a transplant ward.

A chaplain comes into the room. Sontag is polite, which is to say she does not laugh in his face or argue him to the ground. After he leaves she says, "He was kind of cute."

Peter sometimes takes her outside in her wheelchair. By this point she's so weak, and her muscles so wasted from being in a hospital bed, that it is hard for her to roll over, so getting into a wheelchair is a production. But on nice days he rolls her to the lake and they see the ducks flapping around.

She loved being outside. She loved the air. The great civilized world, Rome, Paris, Kyoto, Sarajevo ("I switch countries as easily as other people change rooms," she once wrote), had shrunk to her hospital room. At home in London Terrace, there would be the week's schedule pinned to her refrigerator, packed with operas, plays, movies, music, dinner, friends. Before she got sick, even her younger friends had trouble keeping up with her; everyone who knew her was dazzled by her energy, by her "avidity," to use one of her words. Peter recalls researching *The Volcano Lover* and, it being three in the morning, suggesting they go to sleep and resume the next day. She turned to him and marveled, "Why? Are you tired?" In her thirties, she wrote in the notebooks, "Is being tired a spontaneous complicity with death—a beginning to let go?"

Once it gets too cold to go outside, Peter wheels her down the long hallways of the hospital. By this point it's a huge production to get her out of bed, into the wheelchair, covered in blankets, but it's good for her to leave the room. Sometimes they go to the hospital's zen café for a change of scene.

Her room looks like an operating theater. In order to protect her radically suppressed immune system, everyone who enters wears a robe, a mask, gloves. There is a layer of plastic, of paper, of rubber, between her and everyone else.

In late October, Peter brings a paperback of *The Death of Ivan Ilyich* to the hospital. He is often there for twelve, sixteen hours, and so when Susan sleeps, he sometimes reads. She asks him what he is reading, and when she hears what it is she asks him to read it aloud to her. He brought the book deliberately so that this would happen. He wants to give her an opening to talk about the vast, taboo subject of death, if she wants to, that is.

Sometime over the next couple of days he reads, "In the depths of his heart he knew he was dying but, so far from growing used to the idea, he simply did not and could not grasp it."

Susan loves the part where Ivan Ilyich puts his feet on his young servant's shoulders to make himself feel better. She does not say anything about the part where Ivan Ilyich dies.

Forty years earlier, she had written in her notebooks: "The density of Ivan Ilyich comforts me—makes me more present to myself, stronger."

In the hospital there are floors for people at different stages of recovery. In the ecosystem of the ward, it is very important to move to a better floor. During the five weeks Peter stays with her, he works hard to get her to sit up in bed, to get her to the point where she can get out of bed herself. He pushes her to do it, and eventually she can. Finally they're moved to another floor. Susan is elated. This is progress, this is recovery.

They also keep careful track of the blood work, which measures "the blasts" in her blood. The news in the blood work is not always good.

The transplant has only the slimmest chance of success. For one thing, Susan is seventy-one. With her exhaustive research she knew how slim her prospects would be. On the other hand, of course, she has survived against very, very shabby odds before. There is one person, at the tail end of the bell curve, who survives under the direst prognosis, and she could be that one person, the exception. She has always been the exception. So in a way the slimness of her prospects only confirmed the role she has carved out for herself: the survivor. Dr. Nimer said to David later, "She was not ready to die. As far as seeking treatment, I knew from the first time I met her that she would rather die trying."

To an outside observer, the suffering often seemed like too much to endure. But Sontag had prided herself on not caring about suffering. In a letter to a friend in December of 1998, during her second bout of cancer, she wrote, "The chemo, plus radiation should be over in late February. However much of an ordeal the treatment is, is irrelevant. All that matters is will the treatment work (prevent a metastasis)? We shall see. . . . I don't dare to be optimistic, but I am hopeful. Anyway, by March, I hope to be back to writing, finishing, *In America*." These are the words that stand out to a more ordinary person: "However much of an ordeal the treatment is, is irrelevant."

———

As it begins to seem like the transplant has failed despite its spectacular hardship, some of the people around her are having conversations that open with "what if." For instance, Sharon and David discuss what if someone had talked Susan out of going to Seattle in the first place. Sharon writes in an email: "Even if that had been possible, which I don't think it would have, it would have ended up in guilt about not having given her the big chance. She would never have written off the hope that Seattle seemed to offer."

Slowly, the knowledge seems to come into focus: The transplant is not working. Those around her have on some level absorbed this fact before the official announcement, though she herself has not. The night before the doctors are going to give her the news, Peter and David talk about it over a drink in the suite at the Marriott.

The next morning, the whole six-person medical team comes into Sontag's room to tell her that the transplant failed. Out the window you can see the lake under a veil of heavy mist. David is in the room with her, along with Peter. She screams, "But this means I am dying!"

The doctor's assistant, Juan, a handsome man in his thirties, of mixed Argentinian and Italian descent and of whom Susan is particularly fond, said, "You might want to take this time to concentrate on your spiritual values."

Sontag snapped, "I have no spiritual values!"

"You might want to take this time to be with your friends."

"I have no friends!"

The next day Annie flies out to see her.

When Susan was sixteen, she wrote in the notebooks, "It is a bullying fear of death, the stretching, the straining to comprehend the incomprehensible . . . 'I will die too' . . . But how is it possible for me to stop living . . . How could anything be without me?"

———

The day of the transport the sky is dark, roiled. The wind rumples the hair of one of the medical personnel as she moves toward the nose of the ambulance plane; the tarmac is slick with rain. Sontag lies on the gurney under great waving white sheets, eyes closed, hair snowy, face swollen beyond recognition. There is a majesty to her reclining figure, like she is a queen. This is Annie's photograph of the transport out of Seattle.

Annie has another picture in her head when she brings Susan home. She wants Susan to die in her own bed, in the arms of those who loved her. Peter has that same picture in his head. He imagines her dying surrounded by friends, books, by the paintings that she loved. Sontag herself imagined a slightly sharper iteration of this deathbed scene in "Debriefing": "You were at least supposed to die in a warm bed—mute; surrounded by the guilty, clumsy people who adored you, leaving them frustrated and resentful of you to the end."

But they are not going home. They are going to Sloan Kettering, where Dr. Nimer has another treatment, or several other treatments, lined up.

Once they arrive, Sharon writes an email to David: "Hey, it's not so bad. The trip from Seattle in the ambulance plane was a big success. The attendants were two of the coolest people I've ever met. They kept her doped up on morphine, among their many other sterling qualities. . . . In the meantime, Susan looks like a corpse that's been dead for several days. But she's got most of her marbles when the occasion arises. . . . xxxx Sharon."

The next morning, in her spacious double room at Sloan Kettering, Susan seems to have risen phoenix-like from the grave. She is sitting up in her bed, reading *The New Republic*, complaining about one of the articles. It's impossible to imagine her doing this forty-eight hours earlier. She is a different person.

———

Susan calls Sookhee. "Bring me some of your spicy steak and spinach." Sookhee says, "They're not going to let you eat that stuff, Susan." Susan says, "You hide it and sneak it in!"

There are drugs to put her to sleep and drugs to wake her up; drugs for the pain and drugs for anxiety. It is hard to know how she is underneath the narcotics, or without them, or if that is even a question one can ask. Late into the night, Sharon reads to her from Leonard Woolf's memoir. Her mind is clearly selecting: She has trouble remembering what Dr. Nimer said twenty minutes before, but she knows all sorts of arcane trivia about the Webbs and Chesterton.

Peter brings in Buddhist prayer flags for decoration. Annie brings in a Buddha head, also for decoration. They are both trying to make the hospital into something other than a hospital.

In the meantime, there is the question of what to tell people. There is an official line, and the official line is not exactly the truth but something closer to the heroic medical battle Sontag had mapped out in her head when she was well. They tell callers like Barbara Epstein, one of the founding editors of *The New York Review of Books*, and

Stephen Koch that Susan prefers to be treated in New York, that at this point they can do the same treatments at Sloan Kettering that they can do in Seattle; they do not say that the transplant failed. They are, in fact, giving the impression that the transplant didn't fail. "Maybe it doesn't matter," Sharon writes to David, "but you know what the jungle drums are like." Some of this editing of reality is a concern for Sontag's privacy; some perhaps reflects the magnetic force field of Sontag's own view, or what those around her perceived to be her view: the wild and implausible upholding of optimism, the stubborn defiance of death. The narrative is that she is *recovering*, and that narrative cannot change. Sooner or later, this causes anxiety for most of the people around her, because her place in that narrative cannot change. She is stuck there, fixed there, like a bug in amber, and there will be some speculation, some unsettling imaginings and suspicions that she is no longer the person who wrote that version, the brilliant, resourceful theoretician of perpetual recovery.

And indeed the treatment continues. There is no question of simply keeping her comfortable. David and her doctors are considering experimental drugs. Sharon Googles two of the drugs that have been discussed, Zarnestra and clofarabine. She writes an email to David: "They both seem kind of fabulous . . . what if this stuff works?" On some level they are all still waiting for the magic bullet, for the moment where Susan rises from the hospital bed and is fine. On some level they are in awe of her will, in thrall to it. It is impossible to imagine that she will die; she has been for so long the person who doesn't die.

There is tension now among David, Annie, Sharon, Peter, and others. Some of the private nurses notice bickering; they walk into the room and sense a poisonous atmosphere. There are quarrels that flare up, and there are quarrels that don't flare up but are glowing beneath the surface. There are those who think that Susan shouldn't be in a hospital, that the treatment has gone too far, and those who think that it is important to honor her wishes, and that her wishes are to fight to the end. Ultimately, the legal and medical responsibility lies with David. He does his best and berates himself for it. He tells himself, "She has a right to her own death."

Very few people talk about David and Susan without commenting on how difficult it would be to be the only son of such a powerful and demanding mother, especially one who seemed, over the years, to vacillate between possessing him entirely and abandoning him. Sontag wrote about her own mother's "narcissism, absences, inability to nurture." Her father died when she was five, so her mother was intensely reliant on her intelligent daughter. Sontag wrote, "I played the shy adoring boy with her. I was delicate; the boyfriends were gross. I also played at being in love with her (as when I copied things from *Little Lord Fauntleroy* . . . like calling her 'Darling')." She also wrote, "From Mother, I learned: 'I love you' means 'I don't love anyone else,'" and she may have passed along the same rigorous, punishing standard to David. She brought him everywhere as a date, a confidant, a friend, to parties, dinner parties, screenings.

When he was five she wrote, "I dreamt last night of a beautiful, mature David of about eight years, to whom I talked, eloquently and indiscreetly, about my own emotional stalemates as Mother used to talk me—when I was nine, ten, eleven . . ." She was analytical enough to know that what she was doing would harm him but not generous enough to stop. Even her most loyal friends saw the tangle of their relationship and worried about how some of the more brutal things she wrote about him in the journals—like how as a child he wasn't as intelligent as she had been—would affect him.

David, however, is not interested in their sympathy. He has moved on—at least he had moved on, until this latest illness. He has left the circles where people would be enchanted or enthralled by his mother; he has moved into a world of foreign policy, human rights, a world she was interested in but not entirely absorbed by. He is literally in flight in the sense that he travels constantly. He is like his mother, changing countries as easily as he changes rooms.

———

Peter, who is not coming often now, because he feels increasingly alienated and burned out by the situation, brings her *Persepolis*, a graphic novel written by an Iranian woman, Marjane Satrapi,which he knows will interest her. She consumes it in ten minutes; he wonders if she has taken it in. David reads to her from Byron's *Don Juan*, because he thinks the pacing will keep her attention, because the cadences keep you going.

The room is a double room, meant for two people, so there are two beds, two rolling tables, two side tables, and they are quickly colonized by the laptop, the printer, the Ethernet cable; the room is, even now, part office.

In the notebooks, Susan writes extensively about the "theme of false death in my work." And indeed her fiction is filled with false deaths, with resurrections, with people who turn out to not really have died. In *Death Kit*, in *The Benefactor*, in *Duet for Cannibals*, people who have died pop up again literally as in a cartoon: "Surprise, here I am!"

Sontag traces this interest in fake deaths back to her father. He died when she was five. He was a fur trader in China. She barely knew him, but the idea of his death, so far away, in a storybook world, was not convincing. It somehow didn't *take*. "It seemed so unreal," she wrote. "I had no proof he was dead." For years she dreamed that he would knock on her door.

A series of private nurses have been hired to take care of her in Sloan Kettering. Susan is very comfortable with one in particular, an older black woman named Edaline Cross. Edie would say later, "That woman did not want to die. She did not want to go into God's arms. I can tell you that. I've seen a lot of very, very sick people. And that woman wanted to live."

When Susan was a child, she had been told that her father died of pneumonia, but when she was nine or ten she peeked at her own medical records and read that he had died of tuberculosis. This revelation had an unsettling effect on her: It made her feel like the facts were slippery—this one death, still mysterious, still more fable than anything else.

In her journals Sontag writes of conceiving of her novel *Death Kit* in a flash, whole, when her friend Richard Howard reveals a nickname of his: "Diddy." Sontag writes, "Diddy. Daddy. That's the source of the meditation of death I've carried in my heart my whole life. Diddy is 33 years old. So was Daddy when he died. Did-he? Did he die? The theme of false death, la mort équivoque, la résurrection inattendue [*'unexpected'*] in all my work—" How powerful can that theme be? What form does it take when one lies in a hospital bed in the throes of Vicodin or Percocet or morphine? *La mort équivoque:* the idea, deep down, that one comes back. Was it possible that Sontag, who had made a career of being the exception, of rising above, in some corner of her soul believed that she was never going to die? There are so many ways she has done and undone death in her novels, in her notebooks, in her essays: Heavy, romantic, perfumed, *la mort équivoque* is one of her favorite story lines.

Late one night with Sharon, Susan sits up in bed, telling stories about Hannah Arendt and Jeanne Moreau, sometimes conflating the two. She can't, however, sort out what happened in her hospital room earlier that day. Sharon reports to David: "I left around 1am, with some difficulty, since she wouldn't stop talking. It's her way of keeping her head above water, which is very touching, and certainly better than the querulous kvetching, and in an odd way more alarming."

Peter feels that because of his hospice work, because she knows about how many deaths he has seen, she might open up to him about death. He tries to create openings where she can talk about it. But she never talks to Peter about dying. She sometimes uses a euphemism: "I don't know if I am going to make it." But she never once talks directly about the possibility that she will die.

Peter found the scene at Sloan Kettering demoralizing; he thought, If this were my mother, this is not how I would want her to die. In his view Susan was a tough character, she knew what she wanted, and there was no way anyone on earth could stand up to her. But he wondered if they should have tried. He wondered if they should have taken her to a transplant ward before she had the transplant, so she could see what it looked like. He knew David believed he was following her wishes, but could her wishes have changed? He didn't say anything to David. He thought about saying something, but he didn't.

David, though, was busy arguing with himself. He relentlessly questioned his choice to promote a hope he didn't privately believe in. David himself put it this way in a piece he wrote about it: "I find myself wondering whether the false hope those close to her strived so hard to provide her with in the end consoled her or just increased that isolation."

David also put it this way: "To go on living: perhaps that was her way of dying."

———

Anne Jump also comes to see her a few afternoons a week. Anne is dark and pretty and somehow manages to project extremes of both competence and fragility. Does she bring fresh winter air, like Ivan Ilyich's young servant? She brings news of the world, correspondence. She is the last tether to the regular, working world. She brings the introduction of the Icelandic novelist Halldór Laxness's book, which Sontag is working on. There is still the work. Is she really writing? Anne says that she is. Others say she is not "the full Susan." But everyone recognizes the importance of Anne coming in. Anne does not always want to come in. She is twenty-five, and she is feeling the strain of the job.

Sontag sits fiddling with the Laxness introduction the way she fiddled with everything: "Imagining the exceptional, often understood as the miraculous, the magical, or the supernatural, is a perennial job of storytelling." She was always rejiggering. She was the person T. S. Eliot had in mind when he wrote: "time for a thousand visions and revisions." She would work steadily through the galleys—never finishing, always inside the work, tinkering. David points out she never said "my work," always "the work." And that was it: *the* work, the article "the" itself lifting the words on the page above their petty human origins. (One can't help imagining the tangled quandary for the son, who might have work of his own, work that wasn't "the" work.)

Sontag had always worked in extremis. When she was receiving a round of chemotherapy for her breast cancer, in December of 1976, she was determined to finish *On Photography* by the beginning of January, and she did. During the entire ordeal of her first cancer, she was working her way toward the way to write about it; she was grappling with questions of craft. In the thick of the treatment, she wrote, "I know how to do 'I' now, impersonal, not autobiographical."

And so from her hospital bed she wrote the Laxness introduction: "Time and space are mutable in the dream novel, the dream play. Time can always be revoked. Space is multiple." By the end she was changing words back and forth. This was how she always worked, though. And, of course, for a certain kind of person there is something life-affirming about introducing an experimental Icelandic novel, ushering it into the world.

When Susan was very young, she wrote to a lover, "You must live in terms of dying, Irene, in terms of the pounding imminence of the cessation of your life."

Throughout her casual jottings, you see the thread of not believing in a death, not accepting it, as if one has a choice. In a letter, she wrote about her French editor: "I didn't call Paul Flamand when I was in Paris but of course I am eager to know what's happened to the French translation of *Death Kit*. . . . It's still hard for me to believe that Monique is dead, and I guess one of the reasons I didn't call Flamand myself is that such a call would have made Monique's death more real to me." This is trademark Sontag (not the Sontag of *Illness as Metaphor*, who dealt in hard truths, but the wilier, wishful Sontag of the novels and notebooks), this magical thinking: that one can unmake a death, that one can render it "not real," that one has the option to accept or not accept it.

Many years before she was diagnosed with breast cancer, Sontag wrote in the notebooks: "Thinking about my own death the other day, as I often do, I made a discovery. I realized that my way of thinking has up to now been both too abstract and too concrete. Too abstract: death. Too concrete: me."

———

Once she begins the new protocol, with the drug Zarnestra, the symptoms are bad. She is nauseous, and then the anti-nausea pills knock her out. There is very little life in between. On Tuesday, December 14, she tells Sharon she is afraid. She does not tell her what she is afraid of. She tells her that she "wants to be out of this place." Sharon wonders what she means by this place: the hospital room or something bigger.

One of the private nurses, who is from Guyana, holds Susan's hand for much of the night. She also reads Susan's book *Regarding the Pain of Others*. The nurse tells Susan she wants to read more of her books. Susan says she can't breathe. Dr.

Nimer watches her breathe in her sleep, and her breathing is fine. The doctors conclude that the feeling of not being able to breathe is a panic attack.

At some point in these last weeks, Sontag stops asserting her presence in the clear and powerful way that she was used to asserting her presence. Her presence is instead filtered through the observers, the people who love her, who mean well and have different and conflicting interpretations of what would be best for her. They sometimes refer to her in the third person, in her room, while she is there. She wrote about this condition brilliantly in "The Way We Live Now," where the AIDS patient is refracted through the voices of his friends. "Quentin said, according to Max, what he likes best is chocolate. Is there anything else, asked Kate, I mean like chocolate but not chocolate. Licorice, said Quentin." The voice of the patient himself is lost, subsumed in the chatter and report of others. "The bad news seemed to come almost as a relief, according to Ira, as a truly unexpected blow, according to Quentin." This is the radical loss of self, the truth seeping out into others' perceptions, that Sontag foresaw and understood in her first illness and that she evoked so masterfully in the very syntax and structure of the story. One thinks of Auden's line about Yeats's death: "He became his admirers."

A few days later, on December 16, Sontag tells Sharon that she feels terrible and doesn't know what to do. When Sharon says that the Zarnestra is supposed to halt the progress of the disease, Susan says that if these are the side effects, she isn't sure that she can bear them, and Sharon thinks that by "side effects" she means her deteriorating mental state.

Sharon spends many nights in the hospital. She often comes at 5:45 P.M. and stays until midnight, or she stays later. She is in the hospital room, night after night, and somewhere in these final weeks, Sharon comes around to the view that the treatment is too much. "The nurses would come in and it was a kind of torture," Sharon says. "They would try to give her the drugs, and she had thrush and she couldn't swallow." One time she is wheeling Sontag through the long hallways to get an emergency MRI in the middle of the night. She's starting to think it's possible that the person who wanted to fight to the end in May could not have foreseen the suffering she would go through in December. She is starting to think it's possible that the person who made the decision in May is no longer there.

David has a different view of his mother's commitment to continuing treatment. As he later wrote in an article, "I do not regret trying to get her to swallow those Zarnestra pills even when her death was near, for I haven't the slightest doubt that had she been able to make her wishes known, my mother would have said she wanted to fight for her life to the very end."

At this point, Susan wants drugs that will knock her out, but she is harder and harder to knock out. She starts to talk about Churchill's memoirs, and when Sharon asks what she's saying, she says she doesn't want any "conversation." Later she says she was just "muttering." She knows, in other words, that what she is saying doesn't make sense. That night she dreams that Hitler is chasing her. The nurses and doctors think that she should be distracted, but Sharon writes to David, "She doesn't seem very distractible to me. Susan is a pretty fierce character, and that hasn't changed."

Peter, David, and Sharon all think that she may be talking to the private nurses about dying. The nurses are warm, maternal, religious; they are with her in the middle of the night, holding her hand. The nurse from Guyana says that some of her patients begin to talk to her about dying, at three in the morning, in the fluorescent glow of hospital night, but Sontag never does. She talks about getting better. She talks about overcoming the disease, about remission; the closest she comes to talking about dying is when she says, "Will this work?" but she never directly raises the issue of what will happen if it doesn't. She tells the nurse that she wants to get back to her writing. She gives her some of her books.

On December 18, Sharon is surprised to see that Sontag is being extra pleasant to an excessively talkative nurse she doesn't like much. But then it turns out that Sontag has a paranoid delusion that the nurses have convened a secret meeting and decided she is mean and arrogant and they won't attend to her. In response she has decided to be overly nice to the nurse taking care of her.

Someone goes to buy the best pillow at Bed Bath & Beyond. There somehow isn't time to step back and reflect, even if one were so inclined. The larger issues vanish into the to-do list, the million minute maneuverings to make Susan feel better, the cash to tip the nurses, the quest to obtain the right kind of wet tissues that the nurses like, the endless things to get done. There are no larger issues.

———

The phone rings at Peter's East Village walk-up at seven-thirty in the morning. He is asleep on the futon, but when he answers, it is Susan.

"Come up here." "What's going on?" "Just come."

He gets to her room by eight-thirty. She is agitated. She asks if there is anyone else in the room. He says no. She says that she wants to pray. He suggests the Our Father.

She says, "Why can't it be Our Mother?" He says, "Sure. Our Mother."

And then she runs through it. "No ... patriarchal, Judeo-Christian ... Let's stick with Our Father."

So they begin: "Our Father, Who art in Heaven, hallowed be Thy name ..." Peter considers whether this is the drugs. He is sure the others would think so. "Thy Kingdom come, Thy will be done, on earth as it is in Heaven."

He decides later that it was some statement of emotional need, if not belief. He thought she was saying to him that she wanted comfort. After the Lord's Prayer, they do a Buddhist prayer called the four thoughts, which lead to renunciation. And then she seems satisfied, calmer. Very quickly, though, the natural flow of events at the hospital intrudes. A nurse comes in to check something.

Any conversation is broken off by a nurse coming in; any moment of drifting thought is cut short: Your thoughts are not your own in a hospital; your thoughts belong a little bit to the nurse who is coming to check something.

A few days later, Sookhee sits with Susan, holding her hand. She can't talk at this point, so Sookhee says, "If you want me to pray for you, squeeze my hand."

Sookhee believes that Sontag squeezes her hand.

Sookhee says, "Lord, I am asking you to give Susan peace. She needs peace in whatever situation she is in. Touch her body, Lord, touch her mind, touch her spirit, Lord."

Sookhee thinks that Susan wants to hear her pray. Others might think that Susan just wanted to squeeze her hand, or they might think, *Too abstract: death. Too concrete: me.*

When Susan was in Europe with Leon Wieseltier, he was shocked that she would take communion in a Catholic church. But she was up for anything, a tourist, an adventurer, a dipper of toes in strange worlds. She did not believe in the body and blood of Christ, but she wanted to see what it was all about.

She once went with Peter to a Tibetan prayer meeting. She took notes very seriously the whole time, but afterward she said, "He was very charming, but, my God, what nonsense!"

Sharon asks Dr. Nimer if there is any medical possibility of taking Susan home to Chelsea. Dr. Nimer says that if she left the hospital she would be dead before she got there.

David cancels a Christmas vacation he was planning with his girlfriend. He imagines a conversation he could have had with his mother if it were ever admitted between them that she was dying. In this conversation he would ask her questions about some of the decisions she made. By this he means some of the decisions she made about him. He would tell her he loved her. He can't tell her he loves her, as things stand, because this would mean admitting that she is dying.

But does this final conversation that everyone imagines with a dying parent exist, this moment of perfect closure, the last thing you needed to say coming out whole and entire? Or is it just a fantasy thrown up by a desperate mind, an unobtainable mirage, glittering water in the desert? If you had this conversation, would it be satisfying? Or would it be one conversation in a lifetime of words; would it be, like every interaction we have with someone who is leaving us, *not enough?*

What is not said matters, though; it accumulates and matters. In her autobiographical story, "Project for a Trip to China," Sontag wrote an elegant line about her own mother: "After three years I am exhausted by the nonexistent literature of unwritten letters and unmade telephone calls that passes between me and M."

Sontag and her beautiful mother were sometimes mistaken for sisters. She remembers her mother waking up at 4:00 A.M. in an alcoholic stupor. "I was my mother's iron lung. I was my mother's *mother*," Sontag writes. "I despised myself for my fear of my mother's anger. For my uncontrollable cringing + crying when she raised her hand to strike me."

David remembers his mother's mind ranging to her own parents in the last weeks. Did she think about her own mother's death? Her unhappy, withholding mother. As her mother was dying, her last words to Sontag were, "What are you doing here? Why don't you go back to the hotel?"

On Christmas Eve, Sharon emails David that Susan had been cranky and mumbling the day before. The nurse·was insisting that she swallow the Zarnestra, which was very painful with the thrush in her mouth. The struggle unnerves Sharon, as its logic has begun to elude her, has begun to seem purposeless. Sharon writes that the only thing she can make out from Sontag's rambling is, "I don't want to die in the hospital."

During her earlier treatment for breast cancer, Sontag wrote, "Being ill feels like a diminishment. I'm no longer the owner of my own body. Can I turn that into a liberation? For a moment I felt myself clad in steel. Let them do with my body what they want. I'm <u>here</u> not there. Catch me if you can."

Time in the hospital is strange; it just hangs there, with no progression of the sun, no night, even, in all that fluorescence, in the nurses ducking in at three in the morning, in tests, and medications, and blood pressure takings. There are still typed-up schedules of her day, though; they are perhaps shadows, commentaries on those other schedules that used to mark her days, the brisk, packed schedules of dinners and talks and theater that used to be pasted to her refrigerator. Annie's office coordinates with Anne Jump, who is still running Sontag's office. These schedules are kept because she doesn't want to be alone. They are also kept to manage the wild and different forms of love that Susan elicits, to order and control the conflicting devotions.

Annie comes on Christmas afternoon with lots of gifts for Susan. But Susan doesn't respond to them, and Annie gives up trying to unwrap them for her.

The last time Susan sees Annie, she holds her sleeve and says, "Get me out of here." Afterward, Annie flies down to Florida to see her father, who is also dying.

On December 28, at three-thirty in the morning, the nurse at the hospital calls Sharon to say that the moment has come. Sharon calls David. She tries to call Sontag's close friend Paolo Dilonardo, who is staying at Susan's apartment, but he has flown in from Italy the night before and doesn't answer the phone, so she goes over, pounds on the door until she wakes him up, and together they go to the hospital. She tries to reach

Annie. When she and Paolo arrive, David, his girlfriend, and Hasan Gluhic, Susan's driver from Sarajevo and close friend, are already there. After a couple of hours, Dr. Nimer comes in and turns the monitor off. He explains that if the monitor is on, people watch the lines on the monitor instead of focusing on the patient. Dr. Nimer holds her hand, her arm. At 7:10 he feels for her pulse. *I'm here not there. Catch me if you can.* She is gone.

They wait in the hospital for a few hours. After desperately scrambling to get back from Florida, Annie finally arrives from the airport. She sits alone with Susan in the quiet hospital room. Around noon, the men from the funeral home come to take her.

# Sigmund Freud

## SEPTEMBER 1939

On an early September day, Freud opens the novel he is reading: "'Wretched weather for drowning yourself,' said a ragged old woman, who grinned at him." The French doors of his study give way to the garden, with its blossoming almond tree.

His study in London is an exact replica of his study in Vienna, Egyptian statues lined up like soldiers in the same order on his desk, same Persian carpet, same shawl thrown across the couch, a re-creation of the old sanctum in this more spacious, beautiful house: someone's generous refusal of change. His famous patient, the Wolf Man, talked about the "sacred peace and quiet" of the study, and now there is a new kind of peace and quiet. The patients are gone, but stacked on the desk are the midnight-blue notebooks with his notes on their sessions.

A few months earlier, during a particularly brutal radiation treatment, Freud had written to his former patient and friend Marie Bonaparte, "My world is again what it was before— a little island of pain floating in a sea of indifference." And now the pain is unruly, would be for most people impossible. His family and friends and doctors urge him to take painkillers, but he refuses anything stronger than aspirin and the occasional hot-water bottle. "I prefer to think in torment than not to be able to think clearly," he says.

The decision to refuse painkillers is difficult to watch; it appears to some to be stubbornness. One of his doctors writes, "What he really requires is some psychological treatment to enable him to make a pact with some other medicament similar to that which he has with aspirin, but I dare not suggest that to him." And it's true that the old man is not exactly suggestible. He has made up his mind about this last stretch. He wants to be able to consider and analyze what remains to be considered and analyzed.

In blooming health, he had written: "Towards the actual person who has died we adopt a special attitude—something almost like admiration for someone who has accomplished a very difficult task." And the accomplishment here, the work, is apparent. The necrosis in his mouth has begun to give off an unpleasant smell. There is a hole in his cheek, as if a bullet has passed straight through. His elaborate prosthesis, which he and his daughter Anna privately refer to as "the Monster," chafes in his mouth. At night, because insects are drawn to the smell, his bed is covered in mosquito netting, which gives it an exotic, transporting, colonial feel, as if he is in India or Thailand.

His dog, Lun, will not come near him; the reddish chow cowers under the table. Freud says that what he loves about dogs is their lack of ambivalence, how they, unlike people, can love without hate, but Lun's unambivalent love has now turned into unambivalent fear. Lun, who lay on the floor of Freud's study as his patients went on with their streams of talk, who lay under his desk as he was writing, who had become, through her presence, almost a part of his work, part, almost, of his thinking, is now out of reach.

This rejection is terrifying, because it is the rejection of the living world, of nature itself. The dog will act on knowledge that the people who love Freud will not act on; they will suppress, overcome, but the dog will not. This is the evidence that death is already in the room. The smell is of rotting, of corpses; it would more decently have waited, but it does not wait.

On nice days, Freud still lies on a chaise longue in the garden. There is a breeze, so he is covered in a wool blanket and wears a hat and vest. He looks distinguished even swaddled in the blanket, somehow manages even now to project some of his famous authority, to impose. He wears his round-frame black glasses, his face bone white. In his novel he reads, "For him the universe existed no longer; the whole world had come to be within himself. For the sick, the world begins at their pillow and ends at the foot of the bed." But this is exactly what Freud will not allow. He will not allow the world to begin and end at the foot of his bed. He will not allow that shrinking, or will allow it only up to a point. He listens to the radio reports of the war. He reads the newspaper and follows the march of the Germans through Europe. He reads letters from his friends and from strangers. Letters find their way to his door at

Maresfield Gardens, in London, addressed only "Dr. Freud, London," which amazes him. There is something magical in this, something enchanted; after the elaborate and petty persecutions of the Nazis, this is part of the way England has welcomed him in.

The novel he is reading, Balzac's dark, hallucinatory *La Peau de Chagrin*, lies folded on his lap. "This is just the book for me," he tells his personal physician, Max Schur. "It deals with shrinking and starvation."

———

In his head, Freud had been working for many decades on ideas of how to die. When his friend and disciple Anton von Freund died of abdominal cancer, he wrote in a letter, "He bore his hopelessness with heroic clarity, did not disgrace analysis." This is, of course, a telling formulation: It means there are ways of dying that Freud felt *would* disgrace analysis. These ways would include not facing scientific facts, denying, suppressing at the end. To engage in fantasies of immortality or to enter into a drugged, woolly state, or to otherwise look away, would be shameful, would be in some way a betrayal of both the poetry and the science of their shared venture.

The ideal Freud set out in this description of Anton von Freund's "heroic clarity" is to see clearly. To be rational. To allow oneself to apprehend, fully and with all the senses. Which is, of course, even harder and rarer at the very end than at other points in life. One can read in Freud's near-constant descriptions of his own upcoming death, in his elaborate set pieces of impossibly comic, wry acceptance, an exercise of this heroic clarity, a gearing up.

He wrote, for instance, in the early years of his struggle with throat cancer: "About my operation and affliction there is nothing to say that you yourselves couldn't know or expect. The uncertainty that hovers over a man of sixty-seven has now found its material expression. I don't take it very hard; one will defend oneself for a while with the help of modern medicine and then remember Bernard Shaw's warning: 'Don't try to live forever, you will not succeed.'" His tone here is light, perfectly calibrated, and his correspondence is filled with statements of a similar tenor. He was determined to play, at least on paper, the role of the cool, unruffled man of science, the rational, bemused intellectual; in the course of his many correspondences, he offered up sixteen different kinds of dry resignation; he was, in his studied, eloquent, playful way, unfazed by death. In the weeks after her father died, Anna would speak of this elegant resignation of his as his ability "to reduce every occurrence to its right proportions."

Throughout his life, even when faced with the most breathtaking losses, he would not allow himself the luxury of rage, or the loosening of control; he would not allow himself any kind of outspoken rebellion against the hard facts of mortality. He reined in his anguish, though his terse, intelligent sentences crackle with it. In 1920, when his pretty daughter Sophie died, pregnant, in her mid-twenties, of influenza, leaving behind two small sons, he wrote to a friend, "For us there is little to say. After all, we know that death belongs to life, that it is unavoidable and comes when it wants." From another point of view, of course, there is *much* to say. But Freud would not say it.

In a letter that same year to his good friend and colleague Sandor Ferenczi, he wrote, "Please don't worry about me. Apart from feeling rather more tired I am the same. The death, painful as it is, does not affect my attitude toward life. For years I was prepared for the loss of our sons; now it is our daughter." What he means here is that he had thought his sons would die in the war and had readied himself for the loss. His faith in preparation is central: Freud's barely submerged premise is that death is something to be mastered, something that one prepares for or practices. "If you would endure life," he wrote in one of his essays, "be prepared for death."

It could certainly be argued that this vigorous and energetic man may have been a bit overprepared for his own death. He began making declarations that he was close to death, or resigned to death, long before he was anywhere near dying. In his thirties, he suffered from various ailments, including what he called a "sudden cardiac oppression," a heart palpitation, which bolstered this belief that he was near death. This heart problem was, for him, "accompanied by a depression of spirits which expressed itself in visions of death and departure in place of the normal frenzy of activity." To his closest confidant of this period, Wilhelm Fliess, he talked openly about his fear of dying, which he referred to as his "death deliria." So the idea that he was dying, or near death, long predated his cancer or seriously failing health. He had, by the time he was diagnosed, thoroughly considered and studied from every angle the prospect of his premature death. His devoted translator, biographer, and friend, Ernest Jones, later wrote a letter attributing this early obsession to a "neurotic horror of old age and death."

Over the years, Freud was very often convinced that he was dying. He wrote to Karl Abraham, "The idea that my sixty-eighth birthday the day after tomorrow might be my last must have occurred to others too." He also wrote, "Though apparently on the way to recovery, there is deep inside me a pessimistic conviction of the closeness of the end of my life, nourished by the never-ceasing petty torments of the scar, a kind of senile depression centered around the conflict between irrational pleasure in life and sensible resignation." Why is resignation sensible? Why is pleasure in life irrational? Freud is so eager to rise above, to conspicuously see and take in the facts of mortality, that he can only classify an ebullient attachment to life as "irrational." Rationality seems to be an expansive, overarching code word here for something altogether stranger and more rare: moderation in one's attachment to life. As if one is supposed to be only *a little bit* attached to life.

In one odd and prickly letter years earlier, Freud got irritated with his very close woman friend and ex-patient Lou Andreas-Salomé for being overly invested in his longevity, for being angry or grieved that he was ill. He wrote in a burst of pique: "I have always found you—I will not say resigned, but at least raised above everything that happened around you and to you, and now it seemed to me you were behaving like someone in a violent fury of indignation. Why? Because I had taken a further step on the stony path which leads us out of this existence?" He goes on to say that he's confused by her reaction; his death, he writes coldly, like everyone's, is wholly predictable. Somehow this chastisement for her outrage, for her raging against mortality, is revealing more of his state of mind than hers: He is angry, almost, at her expression of love. He is adamant in imposing this resignation, this cool, rational acceptance of the stony path that leads us out of existence, on his intimates, because the alternative is unthinkable: to fear death, to deny it, to rage against it, to be, in other words, out of control.

When he was in Vienna awaiting permission to move to England and flee the Nazis, Freud often declared that he was done with life, that the fresh start was wasted on him. While his friends tried to negotiate with Nazi officials for permission to take his papers and library—for which his friend Marie Bonaparte ended up paying an enormous "tax"—he said to Ernest Jones, "If I was alone I should long ago have done with life." But his actions betrayed his irrepressible energy: He studied maps of London, devoured guidebooks, did a translation into German—along with Anna—of Marie Bonaparte's whimsical book, *Topsy: The Story of a Golden-Haired Chow*, about the illness and phoenix-like recovery of her dog, Topsy, and labored away on the first drafts of his controversial *Moses and Monotheism*. He was unable to leave his house, because of the Nazis, and unable to see patients, but his mind was throwing off sparks and casting around for projects. So, though he was undeniably old and ill, the giving up, the retreat from life he spoke about so extensively and persuasively, was not the whole story: It was something more like an official stance.

As he was finally leaving on the Orient Express to Paris, en route to London, Freud dreamed he was landing at Pevensey, where William the Conqueror had landed before being crowned—not exactly the dream of someone who has given up on his kingdom.

In fact, the cool state of being beyond caring that he often declared was belied at times by the warmth of his attachments—that is, by his continuing enjoyment of his many attachments. Once, his former patient the poet H.D. sent him white gardenias for his birthday, and he wrote to her: "Dear H.D., All your white cattle safely arrived, lived, and adorned the room up to yesterday. I had imagined I had become insensitive to praise and blame. Reading your kind lines and getting aware of how I enjoyed them, I first thought I had been mistaken in my firmness. . . . Life at my age is not easy, but spring is beautiful and so is love. Yours affectionately, Freud." He is always imagining this rising above, this becoming insensitive, and then something, like a bouquet of white flowers, a note from a former patient, undoes it; he is back among those enamored, implicated, busy with life.

———

Freud argued so eloquently and constantly over the years for his acceptance of death that his closest disciples, given as they may have been to scrutiny and analysis and second-guessing, were entirely convinced. In his memorial, Ernest Jones would say, "Nor did he in any way dread death. . . . If ever man can be said to have conquered death itself, to live on in spite of the King of Terrors, who held no terror for him, that man was Freud." (Jones here may have been forgetting something else Freud once wrote to him: "The overblown declarations that a death normally evokes have always been particularly embarrassing to me.") But is it possible that death held no terror for Freud? That he did not in any way dread death? He certainly did an excellent job of presenting that impression, even in his most intimate associations. But the sheer number of declarations about how completely and entirely resigned he was to death certainly raise at least the specter of their opposite: It begins to sound as if he was persuading himself. Why get so angry at Lou Andreas-Salomé for not accepting his death? Why is not accepting death so shameful, so provocative, so enraging, if you yourself have truly accepted it?

The answer to those questions may in fact lie in Freud's writing. In his essays, he acknowledges that we can accept death while at the same time not accepting death. There is a difference, in other words, between what we know and how we feel, and of course much of Freud's revolutionary theory was pitched in that very space between the two. He writes in the marvelous novelistic beginning of his 1915 paper "Thoughts for the Times on War and Death":

To anyone who listened to us we were of course prepared to maintain that death was the necessary outcome of life, that everyone owes nature a death and must expect to pay the debt—in short that death was natural, undeniable and unavoidable. In reality, however, we were accustomed to behave as if it were otherwise. We showed an unmistakable tendency to put death on one side, to eliminate it from life. We tried to hush it up ... at bottom no one believes in his own death, or to put the same thing in another way, that in the unconscious every one of us is convinced of his own immortality.

He is, in this passage, giving us the key to how to read his letters, with their wry protestations of rationality: "at bottom no one believes in his own death." What we say to "anyone who listened" is here very different from how we feel alone in a room at night. The gulf between our rational knowledge and our primal beliefs is so great that it is impossible to accept our mortality on the deepest level. Even Freud, by implication, with his graceful bravura passages of accepting death, does not on another level believe in it. The heroic clarity he respects, then, is not entirely possible: It is a goal, an ideal, a place to move toward.

————

When he was diagnosed with a "leukoplakia" in his mouth in the winter of 1923, Freud finally found tangible form for his sense of impending doom. He underwent the first of many grueling operations to remove it. His doctors did not tell him right away that it was cancerous, but he intuited that it was, and the radiation and X-ray treatments they recommended confirmed his suspicions. The fact that his doctors treated him like an ordinary patient, lying to him, obscuring the truth, enraged him: He did not want to be shielded or coddled.

His illness strengthened his attachment to his daughter Anna, made it feel more pressing and necessary to both of them. She wrote to Lou Andreas-Salomé, "You are right. I would not leave him now under any circumstances."

Six years later, at the urging of Marie Bonaparte, Freud decided to take on a personal physician, Dr. Max Schur. Dr. Schur was a warm young internist, with an unusual interest in psychoanalysis. Of course, taking on a personal physician, or *Leibarzt*, involves taking an extraordinary position toward one's health, managing it above and beyond the ordinary person; it is the luxury of the affluent, the privilege of a king, but it is also a statement of power, of intent. In taking on a personal physician, Freud entered into a personal relation with death. He was beginning what could almost be called a negotiation. He asked Schur to promise that when the time came he would help him die, which Schur did. He also asked Schur to promise to be completely honest, which he did as well.

In many ways Freud was the perfect patient—stoic, rational. He referred to himself as Max Schur's "docile patient" and was brave and uncomplaining through even the most florid mishaps of his treatments, through no fewer than thirty-three painful and sometimes botched operations on his mouth; yet in his cigar smoking he continued to elude, to rebel, to court his illness, his future death. He knew that his smoking was compounding his lesions, making them worse, and yet he continued to smoke. As he wrote to a friend very early on in his illness: "Smoking is accused as the etiology of this tissue rebellion." But he smoked through the discomforts and difficulties. At one point he told his friend Sandor Ferenczi that he used a clothespin to pry open "the Monster" so that he could smoke. This innovative, desperate image, which he tossed off lightly, as if it were an entertaining anecdote, communicates more clearly than words his unnatural or overardent devotion to smoking.

One wonders why he had such a strong commitment to smoking, even after his doctors urged him to quit, and the answer is hard to sort out. In part, of course, it was simply a physical addiction, but as Freud's frequent rhapsodies over smoking reveal, it was also much more than that. Freud took up what he called "the sweet habit of smoking" when he was twenty-four, starting with cigarettes and moving to cigars. His father was a heavy smoker, and he himself was soon smoking twenty cigars a day. When his seventeen-year-old nephew Harry declined a cigarette, Freud said, "My boy, smoking is one of the greatest and cheapest enjoyments in life, and if you decide in advance not to smoke, I can only feel sorry for you."

In February of 1923, when he first discovered the growth in his throat, Freud delayed telling the doctors, in part because he knew that they would ask him to quit smoking again. After the cancerous lesion in his throat was removed, he continued to have swelling and lesions and difficulty with the large, awkward prosthesis that was fitted to replace parts of his palate. His smoking intensified the complications and side effects; it led, very clearly, to more interventions and pain. Freud would often say to Schur, "I know what you are going to say—don't smoke." On May 1, 1930, he wrote, "For six days now I have not smoked a single cigar, and it cannot be denied that I owe my well-being to this renunciation. *But it is sad.*"

His health problems, seriously as he took them, never really got in the way of his smoking. As early as 1893 he announced defiantly in a letter to Wilhelm Fliess his commitment to continue smoking after his heart troubles: "I am not observing your ban on smoking. Do you think it is such a glorious fate to live many long years in misery?" This is interesting because it is during this time he developed what he referred to as his "death deliria," a serious preoccupation with the idea that he was dying, and yet even then, or perhaps particularly then, he was not willing to give up his beloved cigars. After he began smoking again, he explained to Fliess: "From the first cigars on I was able to work and was the master of my mood; prior to that life was unbearable." These are strong statements: Life without cigars was unbearable, a misery. From very early on he linked smoking to his imaginative work, to his creative side. It seemed to him impossible to work, to concentrate, to envision without a cigar, impossible, almost, to live. Something vital, crucial, was tangled up with cigars, something akin to identity.

The sensible, scientific response to his medical situation was unambiguous. But Freud continued to elude the sensible, scientific response. At one point, his doctors issued a whole written report of the smoking-related damage to his throat and palate, explicitly connecting nicotine to the recurring precancerous growths and inflammation: "specially noticeable this time is the widespread inflammation which . . . is the consequence of excessive smoking. There is every evidence that the inflammation develops first and that the typical leukoplakia appears as its sequel." The report ended with the admonition: "The patient should be strongly advised to give up smoking." When Schur showed Freud this report, he shrugged.

The shrug is the perfect gesture. Freud's smoking did not have a rationale: It existed outside words. It was itself an argument of sorts, an imposition of personality on the facts. He was responding to the warning by not responding. He would try periodically, in starts and stops, to quit, but it would not be possible for Freud to give up smoking, or he did not want to.

Schur himself was tormented on the question of Freud's smoking; he was too close to Freud, too much under his sway, to insist that he stop, but he was also responsible for his health and knew that his patient should stop smoking. He wrote later, "I asked myself repeatedly whether I was entitled, or even obliged, to insist more strongly on the enforcement of abstinence. Perhaps a personal physician with the detachment of Pichler would have done so. I could not, and in retrospect I realize that I should not regret this fact. It's questionable in any event whether such an attempt would have been successful."

Freud's smoking had many meanings to him. Not only was it radically enmeshed with his creative process, to the extent that he didn't feel he could do any kind of meaningful intellectual work without it, but it also represented for him some sort of rebellion, some wildness, some expression of self he did not normally indulge in. He wrote at one point to Lou Andreas-Salomé, "I can report to you that I can speak, chew, and work again; indeed, even smoking is permitted—in a certain moderate, cautious, so-to-speak petit bourgeois way." Which implies there is another way he would like to smoke. There is an excess, an indulgence, a letting loose of impulse that he craves or saw in his usual way of smoking: the immoderate, incautious, irresponsible Freud.

In this same vein, Freud corrected his early biographer, Stefan Zweig, in a letter: "I feel inclined to object to the emphasis you put on the element of petit bourgeois correctness in my person. The fellow is actually somewhat more complicated; your description doesn't tally with the fact that I, too, have had my splitting headaches and attacks of fatigue like anyone else, that I was a passionate smoker (I wish I still were), that I ascribe to the cigar the greatest share of my self-control and tenacity in work." Of course, soon after writing this, he resumed passionate smoking.

His smoking, he suggests here, is crucial to his biography, to understanding his life and times. Freud is interested in this other story, this story written out in smoke. He is not careful. He is not correct. He is not the punctual, controlled, financially responsible, bourgeois Freud. "The fellow is actually somewhat more complicated." There is the wildness of his passion for cigars: It is the fire, the fuel, the fruitfulness. Elsewhere he calls it his "sin," which is an interesting word choice for a man of science, a man so naturally disinclined toward religious frameworks. The word "sin" endows the habit with a glamour, a richness it might not otherwise have; it is his taboo, his vice, his irrationality, and as such it is crucial to him, it is animating.

Freud liked to call himself an "adventurer." The adventure shows itself in his work, in the gargantuan act of imagination required, but it does not show itself in his life, which was, as Zweig pointed out, largely orderly, punctual, proper. His sense of humor revealed the rogue impulse, glimmers here and there of wickedness, or mischievousness, but he did not live the vivid, expressive life one might imagine in the father of psychoanalysis. His courtship of Martha Bernays was turbulent and a little wild, but after they were married, his romantic life remained, on the surface, quite settled, and he hinted that he and his wife ended their sexual relationship after the last of their many children. His explorations of an untrammeled id and libido were purely theoretical and on the page. Scholars have combed through his life for scandal, for the sexual obsession to be made real, which has led to heated speculation of an affair with his sister-in-law, Minna Bernays, but there is no solid evidence that he acted on any attraction to her, or that there was any attraction at all. The one anarchic thing he did, the one vice he clung to, the one irrational pocket of destructive behavior, the one "sin" he could actually lay claim to, was his cigar smoking. During his impetuous engagement he wrote, "Smoking is indispensable if one has nothing to kiss." Smoking, he suggests, is a substitute for the sexual; it is the expression of the libido.

And smoking was also linked in his mind to certain kinds of love. Once when Anna was away on a trip to Berlin, he wrote to Lou Andreas-Salomé about losing her: "If she really were to go away, I should feel myself as deprived as I do now, and as I should do if I had to give up smoking!" This is a peculiar equation, of course, to talk about quitting smoking in the same breath as surrendering the extravagant devotion of your adult daughter. But they are both forbidden in their way, both complex, fruitful, unhealthy addictions he cannot bear to surrender. Anna never moved on; she never married or ran off with anyone and remained, unlike her siblings, in her childhood home. Freud wrote, in a moment of candor: "Sometimes I urgently wish her a good man, sometimes I shrink from the loss." He was too attached to Anna and was painfully aware of the costs of that attachment, especially to her, and yet he was not willing to release her, to entertain the possibility of her leaving him for a fuller adult life. His willful and conscious cultivation of his too-close relationship with Anna is, like smoking, an enactment of something you are not supposed to do. They are both the impulse not resisted.

On the whole, and apart from these occasional allusions, Freud resisted any sustained analysis of his cigar smoking; it was somehow off-limits, separate from the analyzable world. He analyzed himself extensively in *The Interpretation of Dreams* and elsewhere. But he did not analyze his relation to smoking, complex and impassioned as it obviously was; he did not discuss his continued commitment to smoking even in the face of illness and the explicit prohibitions of doctor after doctor. He seemed to be living the idea that "sometimes a cigar is just a cigar."

There is some question about whether Freud actually ever made this legendary comment in a speech he gave to students at Clark University in 1909. He did, however, carve off cigars as a private matter, something to be kept apart from the interpretive digging of his method, in a letter to Ernest Jones: "If someone should reproach you with my Fall into Sin, you are free to reply that my adherence to telepathy is my private affair like my Jewishness, my passion for smoking, and . . . inessential for psychoanalysis." Smoking, then, is in a special, separate category: He does not want it to be analyzed. It is something he does beyond analysis. It is his own mystery.

———

In a slender, controversial book, "Beyond the Pleasure Principle," which came out in 1920, Freud raised the possibility of a silent drive toward death, a secret desire for annihilation animating each of us. He wrote a line many analysts would resist, finding it too extreme, too sweeping, too unsettling: "The aim of all life is death." And in this strange, speculative work, he began to address the irrational draw toward death, the desire for it, the mysterious attraction of undoing oneself.

In his own life, he occasionally alluded to a despair (or, as he often called it, "indifference") that pulled him in that direction.

When his favorite grandson, Heinerle, died at the age of four and a half of tuberculosis, he hinted at a grief so wild and consuming that he couldn't enjoy life. "It is the secret of my indifference—people call it courage—toward the danger to my own life."

In Freud's lifetime, biographers and other analysts tried to connect his theories of Thanatos—an innate attraction to death—to his own grief or morbidity during this period. They argued that he had dreamed up the death instinct in grief after his daughter Sophie died suddenly of influenza in 1920, out of some sort of depression or excessive mourning, but Freud quickly pointed out that he had shown drafts of the book to colleagues long before Sophie caught the influenza that would kill her, and so they were mistaken.

Still, there was always an undercurrent, an attraction, a despondency that every now and then found voice in his letters and work. There was something in the theory of a death instinct that flickered through his personal writing over many decades, that had already appeared in traces, in shadows. The formal postulation of a "death instinct" is in some sense the culmination of a romantic notion, much like his nexus of romantic notions surrounding smoking. There is a perverse beauty to the idea of the death drive; there is a poetry to this disturbing theory, just as there is a poetry to Freud's reflections on smoking. He found the "death instinct" beautiful, seductive.

Freud conceived of the death drive as a force one is powerless against: "The dangerous death drives are dealt with in a variety of ways ... but in the main they undoubtedly continue their inner activities unchecked." The author of these words is the Freud who shrugged when Max Schur showed him the doctors' report saying he should quit smoking, the Freud who lit a cigar in spite of the doctors advising him not to exacerbate his cancer. There is a sense, in his smoking, in this untouchable, unanalyzable subject, of the death drive continuing its "inner activities unchecked." Indeed, Freud saw himself as powerless to quit, even if he had wanted to, which he may not have in any sustained or convincing way.

Other analysts were uncomfortable with the idea of the death drive. Was it too extreme, too overblown, the idea that everyone is propelled or driven toward extinction? Could it be anything more than a majestic or mythic fantasy? But in a certain sense it doesn't matter. Whether or not the model of the death drive comprises an accurate portrait of the human psyche, it did give an accurate portrait of Freud's personal conflict.

Even though Sophie's death did not feed into the creation of the theory, the analysts and biographers may have been right in their instinct that Freud was in some other, more obscure way writing about himself. Is it possible that there was an extravagant longing for death, a positive desire for it that had begun to fascinate him? Freud wrote of the life and death drives, "life itself is a battle and constant compromise between these two urges," and it seems entirely possible that this battle was something he lived through, something he felt very much at work in his own days.

He did sometimes articulate a fairly straightforward wish for death. He wrote to Stefan Zweig: "Although I have been uncommonly happy in my house . . . I cannot reconcile myself to the wretchedness and helplessness of being old, and look forward to the transition into nonbeing with a kind of longing."

Was he, then, both the good patient trying to gain more time for his work and life and the bad patient smoking himself to death? Were both those drives equally irresistible, irrepressible? Take Freud, sitting in his leather armchair, enveloped in a cloud of smoke; take this erratic, stubborn, glorious pocket of misbehavior, the match moving toward the cigar: It would be too simple to say that Freud wanted to die, but it would also be too simple to say that he did not want to die. He would write later, "Only the collaboration and the conflict between both primal drives, Eros and death drive, explain the colorful variety of life's phenomena, never one of them alone."

For Freud, smoking would represent the choice, the exertion of will on unpromising circumstances. Part of his smoking was a resistance, a rebellion, a declaration of himself. He wrote, "annoyed that the discomfort will not give way, I am again sinning more." He could do nothing about his declining health, but he could smoke. He could assert his power over the long hours of an afternoon. He wrote in "Beyond the Pleasure Principle," "What we are left with is that the organism wishes to die only in its own fashion."

Whether or not this is true of the "organism," it was certainly true of Freud. He was increasingly focused on the issue of control, a control so expansive and consuming it encompassed even the mode or method of one's dying. Freud wanted to choose when and how to die. When Anna suggested that they should poison themselves if they couldn't get out of Vienna because of the Nazis, he was irritated and snapped, "Why, because they want us to?" Freud was in no way opposed to suicide in extremis, but he did not want to be forced to die by Fascists or nature; he wanted to choose when he would die. He wrote, while waiting for his visa out of Austria, that he wanted to "die in freedom," which meant, ostensibly, that he wanted to die in England, away from the minor and major persecutions of the Nazis. But he also meant: "the organism wishes to die only in its own fashion."

———

For a long time Anna thought he might recover. She was used to his heroic recoveries. She wrote later, "It is really not so that we had known for a long time that he would die. He was very ill, but then he had been very ill many times before."

Freud, however, was thinking about death in increasingly pragmatic terms. In December of 1936, he wrote to Marie Bonaparte: "If you, at the youthful age of fifty-four, can't help thinking so often of death, are you surprised that at 80 1/2 I keep brooding on whether I shall reach the age of my father and brother, or even that of my mother, tortured as I am by conflict between the desire for rest, the dread of renewed suffering . . . and by the anticipation of sorrow at being separated from everything to which I am still attached?"

Marie Bonaparte wrote a note to herself at the bottom of the letter. "M.: How beautiful everything is that you say, but how sad!

"Fr.: Why sad? That's what life is. It is precisely the eternal transitoriness which makes life so beautiful." She was making this dialogue up, of course, but he had often expressed this view—in a short essay on Goethe, in his letters; it was a recurring theme in their conversation.

In spite of his increasing preoccupation with his physical decline, Freud does not want to stop working. Over the years and through all kinds of harrowing treatments, he had seen patients, often taking only a day or two off after his surgeries. In March 1939, in his office in London, when he was weak from brutal radiation treatments, he continued to see his patients without interruption. He was a willing patient, able to tolerate a great deal of pain, up for any chance of prolonging his life, as long as that life was productive.

"The only real dread I have," he once wrote, "is of a long invalidism with no possibility of working." The work was worth suffering for; likewise, the discipline and habit of it was sustaining. In some not entirely abstract sense, the patients were healing the doctor.

———

He does not close his analytic practice until August 1, by which time he is undeniably too weak to continue. At that point, he has four analytic patients, who come to the house at Maresfield Gardens, and one training analysis. He records their visits and their fees in midnight-blue notebooks. As he writes to a friend, "With all the resignation before destiny that suits an honest man, I have one wholly secret entreaty: only no . . . paralysis of one's powers through bodily misery. Let us die in harness, as King Macbeth says."

And so, even when he closes the practice, the idea lingers: "Let us die in harness." Though he has stopped seeing patients, he has not stopped working. Freud has always used himself in his work. In *The Interpretation of Dreams*, he analyzed his own dreams and childhood. He has very often been the guinea pig, the science experiment, and his own experience and observations feed right into his theories. So the work he is doing now is the work of dying: He is doctor and patient, subject and writer, analysand and analyst.

Freud seems, at times, to be studying his own relation to life: the subtle and nuanced fraying of the connection. As he had written earlier to Lou Andreas-Salomé: "The change taking place is perhaps not very conspicuous; everything is as interesting as it was before; neither are the qualities very different; but some kind of resonance is lacking."

When Schur comes back from a trip to America to work on securing his own visa, Freud is pale and has lost weight. He is coming to resemble one of the finely carved Egyptian statues he keeps on his desk, all whiteness and angle.

In the winter, Leonard and Virginia Woolf came to visit him. Leonard wrote later: "There was something about him as of a half-extinct volcano, something somber, suppressed, reserved. He gave me the feeling which only very few people whom I have met gave me, a feeling of great gentleness, but behind the gentleness, great strength."

For a very long time, Anna has taken on the role of nurse; in his illness the two have developed a physical intimacy that transcends the more ordinary intimacy he has with his wife. His illness has burned down and transfigured his love and somehow allowed or permitted him to be closer to his daughter, without the guilt or self-criticism he expressed in the past. It's as if he is, in extremis, beyond the conventional structures of family life, outside them. He says to Schur in the last weeks, "Destiny was kind to me, that it also granted me a relationship with such a woman—I mean, naturally, Anna."

Even as a younger man, Freud did not like the idea of prolonging life at all costs. He did not subscribe to any lofty or sentimental ideas about longevity. He did not romanticize suffering in any of its forms. When in 1904 Lou Andreas-Salomé wrote a floridly sentimental poem about how she would like to live a thousand years, even if those years contained nothing but pain, Freud commented wryly, "One cold in the head would prevent me from having that wish."

And yet throughout August he remains committed to his extreme alertness, to the idea of not dulling his consciousness. In writing about the rampant casualties of the First World War, he says, "Death will no longer be denied; we are forced to believe in it. . . . The accumulation of deaths puts an end to the impression of chance. Life has, indeed, become interesting again; it has recovered its full content." In some way it is this "full content" that Freud is chasing in these last days: this bright, vivid, painful awareness.

———

On September 1, Freud reads the newspaper reports of the Germans marching into Poland, and Schur moves in to Maresfield Gardens to attend to his patient. Because of air raids, Freud's bed is moved to a safer part of the house. At one point, they are listening to the radio and the announcer refers to the war as "the last war." Schur asks his patient if he thinks it is, in fact, the last war, and Freud says, "*My* last war." Here is Leonard Woolf's half-extinct volcano—which is, of course, half active. The volcano remains a volcano.

Schur would later write a letter to Jones about Freud's mood: "Freud's attitude toward death changed from a neurotic fear of death to an awareness of the inescapable anger which one has to face with wisdom, resignation and indomitable courage . . . he certainly hated the idea of death up to the very end and was eventually constantly aware of its imminent reality, but the 'neurotic anxiety' was gone."

The previous winter, five days after Freud had surgery and three days after he discovered the malignant lesions had returned, Marie Bonaparte wrote to him about a paper she was working on called "Problems of Time in Life, Dream and Death." She ended the letter saying, "But I want to hear about you soon, and learn that we will still be able to have conversations on this earth, before we go to the hereafter in the Elysian Fields."

Instead of his usual protestations of rationality and worldliness, Freud wrote a playfully posthumous letter: "I've been imagining how I would greet you on the Elysian Fields, after learning of your arrival. It's fine that you've finally gotten here. You let me wait so long, and I didn't get to read your last big opus about time. I'm already quite curious to learn what you've found out about it. Because, as you can readily imagine, conditions for acquiring experience about this strange aspect of our mental functioning are particularly unfavorable in this place. Altogether you'll have to tell me a great deal about analysis." In this vision of the afterlife—one he would have spun out only for Marie Bonaparte, whose frothy sentimentality he somehow didn't mind, the way he minded other people's—he is still working on his theories. He is dead but still working.

Freud is reading Balzac's *La Peau de Chagrin* in these last days. "There is something great and terrible about suicide. Most people's downfalls are not dangerous; they are like children who have not far to fall, and cannot injure themselves; but when a great nature is dashed down, he is bound to fall from a height. He must have been raised almost to the skies."

------

## SEPTEMBER 14

Anna sends her very close friend Dorothy Burlingham, who is in New York, a cable saying that her father is worse and no treatment at present is possible. Dorothy writes back, "It's so sad and hard. I wish the ocean were not so wide and I so far away."

The pain is now debilitating, but Freud continues to refuse painkillers. He accepts aspirin and a hot-water bottle at night. He is having trouble sleeping, which is unusual for him. Here is the "heroic clarity" he wrote about in Anton von Freund's death. The clarity is a willed, arduous clarity, a clarity to be honest, which most of us would refuse if we had the choice. He is choosing not only how long to suffer but also how to experience that suffering. He does not want a dimming or a blurring or a diminishing of awareness. He does not want to sink into the state Balzac describes in the novel he is reading: "Thanks to the material power that opium exerts over the immaterial part of us, this man with the powerful and active imagination reduced himself to the level of those sluggish forms of animal life that lurk in the depths of forests, and take the form of vegetable refuse, never stirring from their place to catch their easy prey."

He has a different idea. Freud had written about his own father, who died at eighty-two, "He bore himself bravely up to the end, like the remarkable man he was," and that is the model he has in his head. It bothered him enormously when his first doctors lied to him about the fact that he had cancer and then later about his prospects for recovery. He had written to Marie Bonaparte the previous March: "One has tried to draw me into an atmosphere of optimism: the cancer is in shrinkage, the reaction manifestations are temporary. I do not believe it, and do not like being deceived." Likewise, he has no desire to avoid or gloss over the truth in this last stretch. He talks to Anna about the importance of "courageously looking life, and whatever it brings, in the eye." In his poem about Freud, W. H. Auden puts this same tendency a slightly different way: "all he did was to remember like the old and be honest like children."

———

## SEPTEMBER 19

Anna sends Dorothy Burlingham a cable, saying her father is wretched and in great pain. Dorothy writes back, "There is nothing to say. One just feels, for him and for you. I feel like Job these days as I look in the newspaper and there is nothing but bad news each day worse than the last."

In London, though, the skies are quiet. The air raids have stopped for a few days.

———

## SEPTEMBER 21

Anna cables Dorothy to say that her father has gotten much worse.

Dorothy writes back: "It's such a terribly cruel world. I've somehow lived with the feeling that your father would always be there—anything else seems so impossible. Such courage and such a wish to live."

———

Freud finishes the last page of the Balzac novel and closes the book. He is not working anymore. He is not reading. He says, "My dear Schur, you remember our first talk. You promised me then you would help me when I could no longer carry on. It is only torture now and it has no longer any sense." Then he asks Schur to talk to Anna about it—Anna, who has become almost an extension of his own body. Schur asks Anna for her assent.

This is a question that is impossible to answer. He does not seem different to Anna, just reduced. She writes to a friend, "His bodily pain grew more and more but his spirit never changed in spite of everything."

At first Anna says no, and then Anna says yes.

Schur gives Freud a third of a gram of morphia. He drifts to sleep. Later, Schur administers more morphia when he becomes restless.

A quiet falls over the house. Freud is quiet under the mosquito netting.

## SEPTEMBER 23

"The organism wishes to die only in its own fashion." As he had written, he died in the manner he chose to die, at the time he wanted to die. He chose and controlled something most of us are not privileged to choose and control. He imagined for himself this death. It looked to others like he had fallen asleep. He stopped breathing in the early hours. Anna wrote, "I believe there is nothing worse than to see the people nearest to one lose the very qualities for which one loves them. I was spared that with my father, who was himself to the last minute." He was so much himself to the last minute that Anna would feel as if he were just off on one of his journeys, with her keeping things in order until he came back.

Right up to the moment he took the shot of morphia, it would almost seem as if Freud were taking notes, organizing his thoughts, readying himself for the great essay he would write about dying if he could sit down, after the troublesome part was over, and write it. That essay, ghostly, unwritten, imaginative, wild, hung in the air in the room by the garden. "We cannot observe our own death," Freud wrote so authoritatively, so convincingly, and all the while he was trying his best to do exactly that.

John Updike

Updike had a bad cold that he couldn't shake. He came back from a trip to New York, in his words, enfeebled and coughing. He went to the doctor, who told him he had pneumonia, and he retreated into one of the boys' old rooms in his seaside home in Massachusetts and worried about being a burden to his wife, Martha.

He wrote to his friend Ted Hoagland that he remembered convalescing as a child as being pleasurable, with his mother bringing him strips of cinnamon toast while he was in bed listening to the radio and reading, but that this time it wasn't like that. Now it was just empty, anxious time.

One of the problems with this convalescence was that he wasn't convalescing: The trouble in his lungs persisted. He was still getting up to go to the drafty room to write on his "word processor." He was working on a draft of a new novel about the epistles of Saint Paul and was about a hundred pages in. He was also putting together a collection of poems, called *Endpoint*. But he was still feeling rotten.

He nonetheless went through with a planned book tour for *The Widows of Eastwick*. He and Martha moved to a different city every night, and he was so worn out he would lie down between interviews.

The winter before, an interviewer called Updike to talk about "nothingness." When Updike came to the phone, he apologized for being out of breath. He'd been playing kickball with his grandsons. "I find when I play kickball, which I did with ease most of my life, that at seventy-five it's a definite strain," he said. "You listen to your heart beating and hear your own rasping lungs. It's a good way to keep in touch with what stage of life you're at."

It should be easy to keep in touch with what stage of life you are at—all it takes is one glance in the mirror—but it slips away, that knowledge, and one floats back into other stages of life. This is a feeling Updike knew well, an essential part of his creative stirring. He wrote a similar scene about his character Rabbit playing basketball at fifty-six, before his final heart attack: "His sweat is starting to cake on his legs, with the dust. He's afraid he's going to lose the rhythm, the dance, the whatever it is, the momentum, the grace."

Updike was not improving, in spite of antibiotics. The week before Thanksgiving he went to a pulmonologist, who walked him down to get a CAT scan. A man in the waiting area grumbled that the author was going first because he was famous. A nurse said to him, "if your wife were as sick as that man, she would go first."

The scan revealed that his lungs were riddled with tumors. He had stage 4 lung cancer. He was seventy-six, but this was still a shock, still sudden. Only a couple of months before, he had been healthy, vigorous, playing golf. In spite of his rapid deterioration over the fall, neither he nor Martha was remotely prepared for this news.

In his novel *Couples*, there is a scene where the thirty-ish hero visits a dying man in the hospital: "he saw, plunging, how plausible it was to die, how death, far from invading earth like a meteor, occurs on the same plane as birth and marriage and the arrival of the daily mail."

In the hospital later that day, Martha took out some proposed covers, in various shades of blue, for his upcoming book, *My Father's Tears*. Updike told Martha he didn't care which one they used. "Call Judith and tell her I don't care," he said. "They can use whatever blue they want." This was unlike him. He had long and lovingly controlled every aspect of his covers.

But if he had succumbed to an entirely reasonable black paralysis, it lasted less than twenty-four hours. When Martha arrived the next morning, he asked her if she had made the call to his editor, Judith Jones. She said that she hadn't. He asked her if she still had the covers, and she said she did. He said,

"Now let's figure out which one we like," and they sat together and talked over the different blues.

After that he asked her if she had a piece of paper. She said that she didn't but he should use the back of one of the cover proofs, because it was white, and she handed him a pencil. He began to write a poem.

———

When his children came to visit him at Massachusetts General Hospital, he was, as his youngest son, Michael, put it, "a good host." The common human impulse to entertain, even in a hospital room, seems to have been especially strong in Updike, though he also saw through the impulse, resented it, examined it. At the same time, he was writing a poem about lying in the hospital, making small talk with visiting children and grand-children: "Must I do this, uphold the social lie / that binds us all together in blind faith / that nothing ends, not youth nor age nor strength, . . . My tongue / says yes; within, I lamely drown."

Once, an enchanted young graduate student named Cathy Hiller wrote a profile of him. She tried to sell it to *The New York Times*, but they turned it down. Updike read it and told her that she had portrayed him as too much of a "sweetie pie" and it was boring: He told her that if anyone was going to be interested, it would be because of the unlikely juxtaposition of the pleasant social surface of his life and the subterranean darkness of his fiction.

The word his visitors during this time use most frequently about his manner is "cheerful." He wrote once about trying to be "droll" in the middle of a very bad asthma attack, struggling for air, in the car with the doctor en route to the emergency room. That was how crucial his social persona was to him: Drollness was more important than air. The protagonist in his little-read and little-loved play *Buchanan Dying* says, "Dying, I discover, is rather like dancing, and not unlike diplomacy; legerity and tact are paramount."

Outside Updike's room, the oncologist asked Martha if her husband wanted chemotherapy. The doctor gave Martha the impression that there was no hope. She said he would have to ask Updike himself. Yet the oncologist gave Updike a far less bleak scenario than the one he gave to Martha, saying that Updike could buy himself a year or at least some quality months. Updike, tears running down his face, agreed to give it a try.

When they got home from the hospital, Martha managed to get Updike, using a walker, up to his office to type the poems. He worked in a series of four rooms, up the back staircase, off a hallway, which had formerly been used as maids' quarters. The little rooms were lined with books; one was for answering mail, one for writing poems and stories, one, with only an armchair, for reading, and one for using the computer.

Updike had to type up the poems himself because his handwriting was too hard for anyone else to tackle; it had never been easy to read, but these poems from the hospital were written in an even more cramped, incomprehensible chicken scratch than usual.

There in the drafty study, the prospect was too daunting. He put his head down on the typewriter and said, "I can't do it."

"Oh, yes, you can, John," said Martha. "Just one more book."

———

The chemotherapy in the middle of December turned out to be more grueling than anyone had thought. He wrote another poem from the hospital, this one about sitting there with the drip of the chemotherapy, absorbing the "babble on TV, newspaper fluff," which was "admixed with world collapse, atrocities." He wrote with something like desire: "Get off, get off the rotten world!" (In fact, in the original handwritten version, he wrote and crossed out that it was "good" to get off the rotten world, revising himself, presumably, into a slightly better attitude.)

Updike's oldest daughter, Elizabeth, one of the four children from his first marriage, visited him in the hospital. He mentioned that he had written a poem the night before. He wanted to know if she felt her life was happy. She'd had a rough patch when she was younger, a bad marriage to a much older man, before her happy marriage to her current husband and before their sons were born. She reassured him that it was, very happy.

———

They were at the doctor's, and Martha got out her appointment book. Updike said, "I'm not coming back," and she put away her book. He did not want to go through a second round of chemotherapy.

He wrote the last poem for the book three days before Christmas. Once, in a *New Yorker* article, he'd quoted the German philosopher Theodor Adorno: "In the history of art, late works are the catastrophes." But the poems he was writing were good. He knew the poems were good.

Before he got sick, Updike had been afraid that he was losing the dizzying talent of his younger prose. A few years before, he'd written to Ian McEwan that while the younger writer had become a star, he had become just an elderly duffer writing irrelevant and boring stories about suburban sex. His tone was light, but he did worry that his style was faltering, that he had lost or was losing his verve, a quickness and lightness of touch. And yet in his new poems, the wily inventiveness, the powers of observation, the sheer gift with words that both his warmest admirers and sharpest critics found astonishing, are all there on display. He had been writing about death since he was young, but now he had a fresh subject: his dying.

———

Updike writes constantly about cheating as an antidote to death; in his fiction it is through sexual adventure that one accesses immortality. One of his characters says of a mistress, "Whenever I am with her, no matter where, just standing with her on a street corner waiting for the light to change, I know I'm never going to die."

The idea that cheating bestows upon its participants eternal life is on the face of it a little outlandish. But there is a certain logic here. If you have a secret, submerged, second life, you have somehow transcended or outwitted the confines of a single life. You are not settled, finished. You start again. You live doubly. You take more than one path at the same time. As he explained in *Marry Me:* "His panting under the effort of running uphill seemed delicious to him ... his renewed draft on life. Since the start of their affair he was always running, hurrying, creating time where no time had been needed before; he had become an athlete of the clock, bending odd hours into an unprecedented and unsuspected second life."

Somewhere embedded in this elaborate argument, which extends over many stories and novels, is the belief that sex itself is about grasping at life, that located in women's bodies is some near-mystical source of vitality. In one story, Updike wrote about bumping into a former lover in a parking lot: "I felt in her presence the fear of death a man feels with a woman who once opened herself to him and is available no more."

In his memoir, *Self-Consciousness*, he explains how he himself had transcended the dread of mortality through love affairs. As a young married father in Ipswich, he had affairs with his and his wife's friends. He writes about one of these affairs: "Its colorful weave of carnal revelation and intoxicating risk and craven guilt eclipsed the devouring gray sensation of time. My marriage, I knew, was doomed by the transgression, or by those that followed, but I was again alive, in that moment of constant present emergency in which animals healthily live." The feeling of immediate emotional crisis somehow negates the "devouring gray" of time spent imprisoned in a single life. "At least for the time being," he wrote, "the dread of eventual death was wholly replaced by immediate distress and emotional violence." The idea, crudely noted, is something like "philandering = being alive."

It's easy to mock or condemn this view, and many have, but for Updike sex was a powerful motor, a creative force. It was the shake-up he was interested in, the flight, the motion, the unsettling of the settled. The destructive and creative power of love consumed him, the idea that you could make or ruin something with it. One of his characters in *Couples* gets a happy ending to his romantic life, and Updike says of him in an interview: "he becomes a satisfied person and in a sense dies." Life here is, specifically, the search, the conflict, the quest, the flirtation, the frisson of sexual longing, the erotic restlessness that carries you to another place. Being happy, being settled, is death.

Updike often wrote about periods of morbid apprehension as "gray" or a "gray sensation." For a writer who was nothing if not preternaturally alert to the vividness of his surroundings, there is a dullness he felt periodically, a loss of color, a blanching or paling of experience. One wonders if this could have been a depression he was fighting off, a descending malaise of some threatening or unmanageable sort, though he worked so efficiently, so functionally throughout, it is hard to credit this theory. In *Self-Consciousness*, he writes: "These remembered gray moments, in which my spirit could scarcely breathe, are scattered over a period of years; to give myself brightness and air I read Karl Barth and fell in love with other men's wives."

After a deep, riveting affair in the mid-sixties with a woman named Joyce Harrington, during which he tried and failed to leave his first wife, Mary, Updike began to have trouble breathing. He described lying on the old floorboards in front of the fireplace in their house in Ipswich, struggling for air. He said that a doctor friend once came home with Mary and, watching him gasp on the floor, observed calmly that it was usually teenage girls who suffered from that particular form of hysteria, and after they fainted (which Updike himself didn't) they were fine. In reporting these events, he was, of course, making fun of himself, exploiting the comedy in a graceful way, but the breathing trouble and ensuing terrors were real. When he left the family, years later, his asthma lifted.

Updike had always had death panics, where he was suddenly flooded by the idea that he was going to die. In an early story, "Pigeon Feathers," he writes of his alter ego, David Kern, as a boy: "Without warning, David was visited by an exact vision of death: a long hole in the ground, no wider than your body, down which you are drawn while the white faces above recede. You try to reach them but your arms are pinned. Shovels pour dirt into your face. There you will be forever, in an upright position, blind and silent, and in time no one will remember you, and you will never be called by any angel."

In *Self-Consciousness*, he describes another such moment, where he is making a dollhouse in the cellar for one of his daughters, under the cobwebs of the low ceiling, and is suddenly flattened by the idea that both of them were going to die. He later put this in a novel: "I would die, but also the little girl I was making this for would die, would die an old lady in whose mind I had become a dim patriarchal myth.... There was no God, each detail of the rusting, moldering cellar made clear, just Nature, which would consume my life as carelessly and relentlessly as it would a dung-beetle corpse." There is a moment in another book when the main character wakes his wife up in the middle of the night in a cold terror about dying, and she says sleepily, "Dust to dust," with a casualness that he never forgives.

Of course, it is sometimes hard to take seriously a healthy young man's fear of death as anything but a metaphor, a useful abstraction, a romantic or attention-getting ploy of some kind, a showy and highbrow form of self-pity, but Updike's descriptions of these panics are so constant, so detailed, so deeply woven into everything he wrote or observed, it is impossible not to take them seriously or to believe, at least, that he took them seriously. He never spoke to Mary about these moods; he was, she says now, "private" about them, by which she means that he poured them into his writing, to be consumed by strangers, but did not discuss them with his family.

———

He said, in his thirties, "Being able to write becomes a kind of shield, a way of hiding, a way of too instantly transforming pain into honey." There is implicit in this description a suspicion of this detached, writerly way of coping, of the sweetness of words, but there is also the sheer miraculous fact: turning pain into honey.

His final illness would test this impulse or capacity in a way that it had not been tested. Over the years, he had dutifully and gloriously turned the pain of divorce, loss, fear, guilt, and psoriasis into the honey of words, but the approach of death, and the dwindling of self, involved a whole other, physically and emotionally trickier level of pain. Was it possible, in extremis, to turn pain into honey? Would that trusted ability still be available to him in the last weeks of life?

Updike once wrote quite frankly, in a magazine for retired people, about his fears of losing his extraordinary style. He refers to his "nimbler, younger self" as a rival writer. He celebrates the lost time when he was young, when his material was "fresh and seems urgently worth communicating to readers." He adds, "No amount of learned skills can substitute for the feeling of having a lot to say, of *bringing news.*"

And yet, after the shock of his diagnosis, he stumbled again on a startling, fresh subject. The poems he wrote in those weeks, many from the hospital, are not exactly poems as much as dispatches; they snap into focus the blurry experience of the advanced-cancer patient. They carry the urgency of his early work, the sharpness and swiftness he was afraid he had lost: the power of having something pressing he needed to say.

A poem in mid-December: He notes that his experience of the CAT scan and needle biopsy is not what you would expect; suspended in the donut-shaped machine, he does not feel dread or claustrophobia or panic. Rather, in the "dulcet tube," he feels a great spreading sense of peace and well-being ("Plans flowered, dreams"). He describes with great, mischievous narrative zest the narcotized loveliness of the moment. And then a few days later the biopsy comes back with the worst possible news; the tumor has metastasized. The ironic slap of this story is Updike at the top of his form. The words are electric on the page, the impatience of bringing news again, of journalistic reports from the places we are most afraid of and curious about, the sheer writerly pleasure of unlikely juxtaposition. It is a variety of excitement that one would prefer not to feel, of course, but he was suddenly accessing something creative, he wrote, as in his "fading prime." The storyteller rises, in other words, from the hospital bed.

On New Year's Eve, he wrote to his editor, Judith Jones: "Dear Judith: Maybe the last thing you need from me is another book. But I knew I had enough poems, and the Endpoint theme came crashing home, and so have pushed myself to take this as far as I can."

———

In the first weeks of January, he was still working on editing a tiny volume of his famous baseball piece, "Hub Fans Bid Kid Adieu," which was being put out by the Library of America. He exchanged letters with the editor there, Chris Carduff. He found this untaxing work soothing, the minutiae of proofreading and shepherding the book into print comforting.

Other than that, Updike was withdrawing from the world. He stopped talking on the telephone. He stopped reading his mail. Noticing this, Martha began to open the mail with a letter opener and leave it for him, but he still didn't read it.

On his bedside table were the two books he was reading, *The Death of Ivan Ilyich* and *The Book of Common Prayer*. He had once written about Tolstoy's vision of Ivan Ilyich's death as "being pushed deeper and deeper into a black sack." He talked to Martha about Ivan Ilyich, specifically about how isolated Ivan is in his own head. There is in that book a slow falling away of the world, a brittle aloneness.

There was also a book he was not reading, Barack Obama's *The Audacity of Hope*, which Martha had given him for Christmas. It lay next to his bed, untouched, until she took it away. She had originally gotten him an Hermès tie on a trip to New York, but that seemed like the wrong gift, so she didn't give it to him.

Martha asked him if he had it to do over again, would he decline the one arduous bout of chemotherapy. He said no. He said he had to do it so he'd know he had tried everything.

———

None of Updike's four children from his first marriage felt wholly comfortable at Haven Hill, the stately house in Beverly

Farms, Massachusetts, high on a hill, overlooking the ocean. Dropping by was not encouraged. It seemed to them that the Updikes spent more time with Martha's grandchildren, rather than his, running through its rooms.

Instead, Updike would come to their houses for tea or meet the grandchildren at the movies. It was their impression that when there was a family gathering, Martha often had an exit strategy, an appointment or movie they had to leave for. Updike wrote in a letter that Martha was uncomfortable with the gatherings of his clan.

When Updike's children called, Martha would often get on the line after ten minutes, apparently needing the phone, and the conversation would end. Among the children, there was a perception that she was policing his time, a perception bolstered by his letters, on which she scrawled angrily at the presumption on his time of various interlopers, from lowly bibliographers on up to Nadine Gordimer. What is surprising in these marginal scribblings is her level of outrage, her protective fury. David Remnick, the editor of *The New Yorker*, would later, in eulogizing Updike, refer to Martha as his "lion at the gate." But even to some of his children, it appeared that Updike wanted or needed that lion there; he was complicit, secretly colluding, complexly involved, as married people always are in these sorts of things.

David, his oldest son, decided to write his father a letter. Elizabeth had told him about Updike asking her if she was happy. This seemed to David a search for reassurance, a request for confirmation that Updike hadn't damaged them with the up-heaval of affairs and divorce. David wrote in this letter that he did feel that he overall had made a good life for himself. This was not a conversation he felt he could have in person. In person there was small talk.

David describes an awkwardness that fell between Updike and his children. Updike himself wrote that after he left the family, he developed a stutter with them, out of guilt or unease, meaning words were literally hard to get out. Updike on the page has an unusually fine or precisely calibrated sense of the deeper emotions, but with his children he seems to have tended toward a deflecting charm, a highly evolved form of shyness.

David attributes some of his father's lack of expressiveness to the old German Pennsylvanian stock, which may have merged with the New England Waspishness that Updike had been cul-tivating since Harvard; feelings were not easily or liberally expressed. Updike wrote about an extreme family reserve in one of his early stories. The character's mother is dying of cancer; on her last visit to her son and grandchildren, "she knew it was the last time but disdained to admit it, as she dis-dained to admit she was dying; she had been a lifelong under-stater; her last words, to the attending nurse and me, were 'Well, much obliged.'"

In the middle of January, David came to Beverly Farms with his nineteen-year-old son, Wesley. Martha had something to do in town, and David and Wesley spent seven or eight hours with Updike. At this point, he was still walking, with difficulty, with the walker, and he came downstairs to sit at the table with them for lunch. In order to make small talk, David asked his father about Martha's family and they talked about her children and grandchildren.

When Updike dozed off, David and Wesley wandered around the big house.

At one point Updike said, "Oh, David, what will become of me?"

———

Having grown up with grandparents in his house, Updike was prematurely engrossed by the various declines of old age. It's a little shocking to realize that Rabbit is in his early fifties in *Rabbit at Rest*, which is a meditation on Rabbit's old age. He might be, like Updike himself at that age, in full bloom, but instead he is old, retired, in Florida, worrying about salty snacks and gazing out on his decline. Rabbit is very much not Updike in that sense, the Updike who would "retire" only weeks before his death, but he is Updike in that he's interested in—one could say almost reveling in—the character of "old man" way before his time. Updike seemed to relish the character of genial, successful old man of letters. He saw a certain doomed grandeur, a ruined beauty, in old age, a richness of experience that he wanted or had to get on the page. For a certain type of artist, the question "Is it fun to be old?" might be less important than "Will it be good to get on the page?"

Asked once about his own parents' reaction to his work, Updike said, "They both have a rather un-middle-class appetite for the jubilant horrible truth," and that phrase—"the jubilant horrible truth"—gets at his sensibility with rare precision. His impulse toward exposure, his brutal accuracy, his honesty about the degrading or harsher sides of life, all tango with joy. One of the great draws and challenges of Updike is that horrible truths are happily reported, reveled in, celebrated, and aging is no exception.

When Rabbit's mother is dying, his father says that "she's having the adventure now we're all going to have to have." The word "adventure" here glows bright with the curiosity that Updike himself brings to the topic. There is an "adventure," an experience that he is hungry to capture and pin down in words; the excitement, the appetite, of the word is what is strange: An adventure for Updike was something to be written about.

A couple of summers earlier, he had written to Ian McEwan about Philip Roth's novel of physical decline, *Everyman*. He said that he felt he had to read the new book even though he didn't want to face death. With the jostling and explicit rivalry between them, he may also have meant, little as he wanted to cede a big subject like that to Roth.

———

He couldn't stand up to shave. Martha's son Ted came for a visit, and he helped him. Ted, Martha's youngest, had been five when Updike moved in with them, and the two had a close, uncomplicated rapport. He told Updike that an electric razor would arrive for him the next day, which surprised Updike, who was not *au courant* on the efficacies of the Internet. When it arrived, Updike was very pleased. He held it in his hands in bed, a small miracle.

———

Martha and Updike were driving around Manchester, which was a nearby town. He waited in the car while she picked up some medicine. "How would you like to drive me to Smith's Point?" he asked, and she did. He wanted to see Emmanuel Church. She went there in the summers, on her own, and was on the church council.

It was a small, pretty, red-brick church with a white steeple. The church had just completed a memorial garden, the ins and outs of which Updike was very familiar with from Martha's involvement. They stood looking out at the simple garden. It had a dogwood tree; in summer, it would have hydrangeas. There were benches, but there would be no gravestones or markers. There would only be small plaques on the church wall. They stood there but didn't say much. Finally Martha said, "How would you like to be buried here?" and he said he would.

He had originally planned to be buried in Plowville, Pennsylvania, with his mother and father, and had more recently told his children he wanted to be buried in Chicago with Martha's family. But this way he would be closer.

Here is a conversation about death that Rabbit's grown son, Nelson, has with his friend Billy: "By our age, Billy, we should have come to terms with this stuff." "Have you?" "I think so. It's like a nap, only you don't wake up and have to find your shoes."

———

Updike's first wife, Mary, wanted to come and visit. Martha told her that, yes, she was on the list of people Updike wanted to see and she could come, but she needed to come with one of the children, so she brought their youngest daughter, Miranda. It was Mary's third visit to Haven Hill. The first had been for Elizabeth's wedding, and the second had been to get some books signed for a friend.

Mary lives with her second husband in the same house overlooking the salt marshes in Ipswich that she had shared with Updike. Photographs from her years with Updike show Mary in black turtlenecks and jeans, with a casually upswept dark bun, chopped bangs, and a warm, open smile; one can see the quiet, artistic Radcliffe girl Updike had pursued. One detects the splendid, sweet, earthy power of his fictional first wives. He wrote about one of them that she was always giving her husband courage and did not forsake that habit even as he was leaving her for another woman and needed courage to do it. In books like *Marry Me*, *Couples*, and *The Maples Stories*, one is struck not by the glittering seductions of the sharp, ambitious, sexually enthralling mistresses but by the deep, agonized love the husbands feel for the first wives, a mystery and softness that Updike could never quite finish plumbing the depths of: It is the first wife who fascinates.

When Mary and Miranda walked in, Mary hugged Martha, who stiffened. Mary and Miranda both sterilized their hands, and then Martha took them into the living room and said he was so weak it would have to be a short visit. Mary was worried that Updike could hear Martha talking about how weak he was, that her voice carried upstairs.

They went up to the second floor, where he was lying in a four-poster double bed in a guest room. He was cheerful and talkative. Mary held his feet through the covers. Miranda stood near the head of the bed. Martha stayed in the room until the phone rang. When she left to take the call, Mary and Updike started talking about the woman who was calling, whom they all knew. Mary said something not entirely flattering about her. When Martha came back in, she said, "We are not here to gossip."

Updike talked with enthusiasm about the Obama inauguration. It was exactly the kind of charged cultural moment that always appealed to him, but Mary felt that he was—that they both were—particularly invested in it because of their three bi-racial grandchildren.

A few minutes later, Martha told them it was time to leave. Updike said, "Remember Aunt Polly." He loved Mary's aunt

Polly, who had lived to be ninety-two, doing the *New York Times* crossword puzzle and reading the news, sharp and independent until her death.

Mary didn't kiss him goodbye. She thought they were coming back. Holding his feet through the covers was as close as she got to conveying anything.

On the way down the stairs, Mary told Martha she wanted to see him again. Martha said no, that this would have to be the last visit. He was too weak.

Over the years, Mary and Updike had talked less and less about the children. She had gone back to painting and sometimes exhibited her work in local galleries. Her paintings are lovely and peaceful; even the urban scenes are suffused with surprisingly hopeful colors, salmons and lilacs and powder blues, making everything look ordered and quietly right. Updike would go to the shows and write his comments in the guest book.

Mary does not indulge the bitterness or hardness or self-protective irony that most people harbor toward their ex-spouses; she does not feel the need to prove that he was at heart a very bad or impossible or fundamentally remote person and she was better off without him. Instead, she projects clarity and honesty in her discussion of him; she has access to a surprisingly uncomplicated affection toward him that is at once realistic and tender. He left her for another woman and then publicly examined that departure for decades, and yet it seems that she accepts him, in all of his glories and limitations, in a pretty rare way.

"I would have loved to have that last conversation," she says, "but there was no way to bring it up without his bringing it up. I didn't want to say I knew he was dying. I didn't want to alarm him."

What would the conversation have been like? In Mary's description, there were still mysteries to be unclouded, history to be straightened out, some of it trivial, some of it not. "There were so many things I could have asked him that only he could answer." But with Miranda there and Martha hovering in the middle distance, there was no possibility of that conversation.

———

A couple of days later, Elizabeth visited her father at home. He told her that even though he was happy Obama had won, he couldn't enjoy the inauguration speech. He felt outside it.

He returned a portable desk with a cushion that Elizabeth had given him to write in bed. He told her he wouldn't be needing it anymore. Elizabeth asked him if he would like to find a collaborator, someone who could help him finish the novel on Saint Paul. He said no.

Updike wrote a short note to Chris Carduff about the Library of America edition of his work saying that he was too sick to go on, and that Martha would help him.

## FRIDAY, JANUARY 23

His old friend Dick Purinton, a retired manufacturing sales rep, came over to stay with him while Martha dipped into town to see the lawyers. He was one of the few friends Updike saw by this stage. Dick was an old golf buddy whom Updike had known since the early sixties; the Purintons lived in a town near Ipswich and had been to some of the complicated parties and volleyball games Updike fictionalized in novels like *Couples*. Dick and his wife were among the few couples who'd stayed together.

While Dick was there, Updike dozed off every fifteen minutes or so, but they talked in between. Dick had brought along a photo album of the trips their golf club, Myopia Hunt Club, took to Scotland and Ireland, and they reminisced. Once a year, Updike went with "eleven other elderly gallants of the North Shore" on a vacation without wives. They played golf and stayed in inns and had long boozy dinners, though Updike in later years didn't drink. Updike's childhood sweet tooth was awakened on those trips, and he bought candy and licorice.

One of the photographs shows Updike on a cobblestone street, in caramel corduroys, a hound's tooth jacket, and a royal-blue turtleneck, his thick eyebrows half concealed by a cap. He looks happy, relaxed, with the slightest hint of slyness, as if he has gotten away with something minor but thrilling. Updike told Dick this was his favorite picture of himself.

What did they talk about on those endless emerald golf courses, familiar and new, over the decades? Sports, sex, nothing. What they didn't talk about was writing. Dick says, "We kind of made a point not to talk about his writing." One of the reasons Updike had left the jostling seductions of New York and the literary world was so he could have golf buddies like Dick Purinton and live a life he could write about and not have to talk about writing.

But now he said to Dick, "I am really angry. I just can't bring myself to write."

In golf, Updike loved to win and hated to lose. They would play for two, maybe five dollars. He liked the ambience of the game. He didn't like caddies and would carry his own bag. He would let out a terrible theatrical moan when he hit a bad shot.

Updike had written whole novels in pencil on yellow legal paper and on the backs of scrap paper, in barely legible scrawl, sentences crossed out and inserted with elaborate trees. He had written poems with drawings and doodles on them, faces and bubbles and shadings and little men, an endless flow of words. Now the writing was over, but the urge was not.

Writing was solace, escape, shelter. Another golf buddy, Dick Harte, remembers one of those trips, walking to lunch with Updike on a raw, drizzly day in Scotland. Updike suddenly turned to him and said, "I just wish I could go somewhere and write something."

It's hard to conceive of Updike as straightforwardly religious, since he was known for rhapsodic philandering, for his risqué explorations. His son Michael said, "It's hard to understand how anyone so intelligent could believe in God." Or maybe it's hard to understand how someone so attuned to irony, and alert to absurdity and fascinated by baseness, could be religious. But in his troubled, intense, intelligent relation to religion, perhaps none of these things were contradictions. In fact, Updike said, "I plotted *Couples* almost entirely in a church—little shivers and urgencies I would jot down on the program." In a way this act, noting down the plot of the story of *Couples*, the prototype for his most famous ode to adulterous adventure, in church, on the program, seems to capture the essence: a faith coexisting with a very American search for self-fulfillment, a kind of rapturous merging of the two. His affairs are tinged with guilt, his sex scenes with heaven, his love with rapture; it's all jumbled together.

About Piet in *Couples*, he wrote, "Prayer was an unsteady state of mind for him. When it worked, he seemed, for intermittent moments, to be in the farthest corner of a deep burrow. . . . In this condition he felt close to a massive warm secret." This unsteadiness of faith recurs throughout his fiction. He narrates terrifying moments of doubt and then moments of return, of flooding grace. In "Pigeon Feathers," the boy begins to doubt: "If when we die there's nothing, all your sun and fields and whatnot are all, ah, *horror?*"

As Miranda put it, Updike loved "the concrete stuff" of the church, the rituals, the Sunday mornings, the church pews. He said the Lord's Prayer with the children in their rooms before they fell asleep. In later years, he and Martha attended services regularly at an Episcopal church, St. John's, minutes away from their home in Beverly Farms. He would go to the eight o'clock service on his own, because it was too early for Martha and she liked the ten o'clock service. When he was too sick to go to church, the Episcopal priest came to his house two or three times a week to talk to him and give him communion.

But even in the months of his dying, his religious feeling was not without irony. He wrote in *Endpoint*, "a clergyman— those comical purveyors / of what makes sense to just the terrified— / has phoned me, and I loved him, bless his hide." One might take this as an expression of skepticism—what makes sense to just the terrified? *Exactly*, a million atheists might agree—and yet Updike approached everything under the sun with irony, including his deeper passions, his beliefs, his sources of marvel and awe. Irony exhilarated him; it breathed life into those passions, invigorated them.

———

How did he feel about Martha, the vivid blond woman he had left his family for in the seventies? She was by all accounts vibrant, forceful, chic. She did not quietly recede, as Mary might have at times. She was fun and charming. She was staggeringly efficient. She was strenuously protective of his time, vigilant toward encroachers. She had taken an English course with Nabokov as an undergraduate at Cornell, and he had called her a "genius." She hungered for travel and warm places.

There is a black-and-white photograph of the two of them, shortly after he left Mary, taken in East Hampton. It is dusk and they are standing in the beach grass, she in bangs, a gypsy dress, a chunky cream cardigan, he in a flamboyantly striped sports jacket; they are holding paper cups, leaning in for a kiss, and there is a great enchantment in the photograph being duly recorded. In fact, I can't think of a single other photograph on earth in which one can so palpably, undeniably, see love.

From his letters, Updike seemed devoted to Martha; he seemed to revel in uxoriousness, take to the role. But it's hard to know what the marriage was like. He was a highly autobiographical writer, stealing liberally from life, so one wonders about his portrait of the marriage of an aging successful man, Ben Turnbull, and his wife, Gloria, living in a mansion on a hill in *Toward the End of Time:* "After a certain age marriage is mostly, its bitter and tender moments both, a mental game of thrust and parry played on the edge of the grave." Gloria is not Martha, and Martha is not Gloria, but they may share certain qualities, or certain qualities of Martha's may be amplified in Gloria. He wrote: "To Gloria I am a kind of garden, where she must weed, clip, tie, deadhead, and poison aphids." Gloria criticizes the way Ben showers, shaves, dances, chooses pajamas, and eats soup. Gloria takes—or, maybe more accurately, vibrantly seizes—what she needs out of life, which is something her husband both admires and is daunted by; he joyously submits to her. Ben Turnbull feels that his fantastically, energetically, zealously organized wife is waiting for him to die, and yet even this is sort of dear to him.

Updike wrote a late poem about a birthday dinner he had with his wife at an inn in Arizona, for "only two." He wrote that they had decided to give up wine and cigarettes to prolong their marriage. He wrote about his "imitation of a proper man" fitting him not like skin but like a "store-bought suit" and working well enough, until she corrects him for not using the finger bowl properly. The scene is suffused with a kind of modest happiness, a peaceful, domesticated warmth, but there is also a tinge of regret, of wistfulness toward another fuller time, other more vivid, crowded celebrations, wineglasses catching the candlelight, other birthdays, maybe happier or more desperate ones. Is it just the closing down of possibilities of getting older he is gently pointing out? Is there something petty or controlling in his second wife, hinted at in the finger bowl? John Cheever once wrote to him: "I thought Martha lovely and I greatly admired her manners. I do like people who know the forks."

After Updike married Martha, the drama shifted from the flashy distractions of adultery to mortality; there was in his later years a fascination with death, which almost eclipsed the fascination with sex. He wrote in a late poem, "How not to think of death? Its ghastly blank lies underneath your dreams, that once gave rise to horn-hard, conscienceless erections."

The mystery is what happened during his relationship with Martha. If these great, blustering fears of mortality were man-

aged and combated with affairs, with myriad free-floating seductions, flirtations, trysts, how did he manage them in the
long, faithful decades of his second marriage? "The older I
get," he told an interviewer, "I'd say I am more monogamous.
Monogamy is very energy-conserving." Looking through his
emails after his death, his children found no smoking guns, no
tangible evidence of any affairs. If he did have a fling far from
home, which he most likely did not, this infidelity did not oc-
cupy or transport or intrigue him the way it did when he was
younger. So what happened to all that energy, the sexualized
urge for flight?

Many people violently disliked *Toward the End of Time*, which
he wrote at sixty-five, but it addresses this question; in a series
of semi-hallucinatory scenes, it offers up the story of an old
man still cheating, still thrilling to the powder-blue underwear
of a fourteen-year-old girl. The scene of the sixty-six-year-old
man fondling the barely teenage Doreen in the woods could be
disturbing, except that it is not a portrayal of a child molester
but a dreamer, a fantasist; it is a scene about being carried back
to a time before he was old. In her review in *The New York
Times*, Margaret Atwood says another mistress of Turnbull's
is either "a working-class slut" or a "superheated fantasy." One
can't be sure. The line between what is in his mind and outside
it is that blurred.

Toward the end of *Toward the End of Time*, Turnbull gets
prostate cancer and is impotent, but the dreams and fantasies,
the scenarios playing out on the screens of inner life, are potent, present, real. Ben Turnbull sinks back into the heated

early days when he was courting his second wife. He gets lost in reveries about a dirty limerick the boys passed around and studied in his school. He is buoyed and buffeted, drifting into the past and then jarred into the present. He thinks, "With a deadly lurch in my stomach I realize I will never attend high school again." The idea of a linear life is something Updike keeps discovering, stumbling into, marveling at; it doesn't come naturally to him. He is so busy undoing it, opening it up, blasting it apart.

The redemption Updike wrote about through sexual adventure would be inscrutable to coming generations and difficult to discuss even for his own. This would not surprise him. He once wrote, "Will the future understand ... how much sex, with Freud's stern blessing, meant to us?" The future, it turned out, would not, or rather would claim not to. It would mock and deride how much sex meant; the future would think itself above or beyond that overinvestment with sex. David Foster Wallace, for one, wrote that Updike "persists in the bizarre adolescent idea that getting to have sex with whomever one wants whenever one wants is a cure for ontological despair." He goes on to say that Updike views Turnbull's "impotence as catastrophic, as the ultimate symbol of death itself, and he clearly wants us to mourn it. . . . I'm not especially offended by this attitude; I mostly just don't get it."

In the impotence Updike extravagantly imagined, there is a fiercely potent mind: "Her tight butternut ass, with its white thong shadow, up in the air, the little flesh-knot between the glassy-smooth buttocks visible in the moonlight that entered the third-story window at just the right celestial angle. The flat planes of her face harking back to the Egyptian Sphinx or some heavy Aztec head of solid sandstone, only transposed to a smaller, female scale, with modern nihilist nerves." He was still playing with words. The idea he was playing with was escape through sex, transport—travel, almost—a mythical transcendence.

Updike's eternal interest in fantasy gets richer and wilder and lusher in his later work. In much of his often-painful writing of old age, fantasy is almost uncomfortably unloosed; in an essay in *The New Yorker*, he quoted Eve Kosofsky Sedgwick, who wrote that in artists' late works "the bare outlines of a creative idiom seem finally to emerge from what had been the obscuring puppy fat of personableness, timeliness, or sometimes even of coherent sense."

Updike wrote to a friend, in 2006, that he had found himself at a dinner party where he was the only person at the table who remembered Pearl Harbor. He said that he had to teach himself that he was an old man. This hints at the impossibility of thinking of oneself as old, maybe even the desirability of losing touch with the current self in favor of more-vivid past ones. Updike's characters are richly attuned to their past experiences. Memory is more vivid in Updike, more intrusive, more gorgeously rendered, than in most people's actual days. His characters swim through dreams, memories.

Whether the encounters in *Toward the End of Time* are real physical encounters is not the point. Updike was writing epic sexual affairs, even if he wasn't having them. The lavish, color-ful, wild affairs exist in the writing.

He wrote in that novel: "I would not die, I realized; all would be well. All the fleeting impressions I had ever received were preserved somewhere and could be replayed."

———

In *Self-Consciousness*, Updike describes himself as "a distracted, mediocre father," which was, according to his children, both true and not true. After he exited the family, in the mid-seventies, to live with Martha and her children, he became dis-tracted and mediocre, but when he was living with them he had his wonderful side.

The children in Updike's novels and stories, especially in *The Maples Stories*, are not shadowy; they are not, as one might think, indistinct blobs one is responsible for while the more interesting business of flirtation ensues. They are lovingly, singularly delineated.

In life, Updike was very concerned about the "black hole" of his divorce, the violence toward the children, which was a large part—though not all—of what kept him from leaving the first time he seriously entertained the possibility. In one *Maples* story, "Separating," he writes a scene that his children say is a very accurate rendering of the night he and Mary told them they were splitting. The parents agree to tell the chil-dren separately, after a celebratory dinner to welcome the eldest daughter home. But as they sit down to eat lobster and drink champagne, the Updike character begins to cry at the table, hijacking the announcement with his own rush of emotion, forcing the Mary character to explain his tears to the children, while he plays for sympathy. The character based on their then-fifteen-year-old son, Michael, gets drunk and eats a cigarette out of grief.

Michael, who says that on that particular evening he did drink champagne and eat a cigarette, talks about how quickly Updike's concerns about the family transmogrified into "a little pity party for himself." Michael remembers him coming by the house to pick up a chair and saying wistfully that now he would have to learn to cook for himself.

But before that year he was, for all his wanderlust, for all the intensity of his drive to write, not a bad or even a mediocre father. When his four children were infants, he woke up in the night and carried them to their mother to be nursed, which was above and beyond for a fifties' father. As they got older he threw himself into board games—Parcheesi, Monopoly—with zeal; he played kickball, softball, something called "roofball." He drew them whimsical birthday cards with their pictures on them. Because he did not go off to the city on the train to work, he was a less remote and shadowy presence than many fathers of that time. David remembers him as unusually available to them. He was not one of those writers who create a sacred, hushed space around writing time. "There was no sense of the preciousness or importance of his time."

Elizabeth remembers him as playful and fun, when you got his attention. "He was often deep in thought, even when he wasn't actively working at his desk," she says. "It could take him a moment to leave that thought and wrap his head around the simplest of questions."

When Michael and Miranda were little, he told them bedtime stories in which an animal in distress seeks out the help of the sometimes-grumpy Wise Wizard. These bedtime stories would later be repurposed in his story "Should Wizard Hit Mommy?" in which a storytelling father becomes estranged from his wife. He deftly used this moment his children thought of as sweet and intimate as part of his rich fictional exploration of domestic ironies, an impulse that they—because they were his children, and artists themselves—basically understood.

As Michael and Miranda got older, maybe nine, ten, eleven, the Wise Wizard got grouchier and grouchier, until one day he was on a beach in Florida, with his long flowing white hair and long white beard, in an orange Speedo, much like one a neighbor of theirs wore; when the wizard got exasperated, his balls fell out of the Speedo. Michael says, "That was very close to the end of the Wise Wizard stories."

———

Updike's daughter Miranda wonders if the cheerfulness, the resolute evasion of his evident decline, was his last attempt at protectiveness, his final act as a father protecting his daughter from the reality of death; it was also in keeping with his notions of stoicism, of not talking excessively about one's fears or pains or fantasies or anxieties. The talk went onto the page. The talk had always gone onto the page.

Updike had long written about stoic virtues in relation to death, which involve not complaining, not kicking up a fuss, not being overly grandiose; stoicism, for him, involved continuing his wryness under duress, not failing to see either the big picture or the joke. He lays out this perspective in *Self-Consciousness:* "Isn't it terribly, well, *selfish,* and grotesquely egocentric, to hope for more than our animal walk in the sun, from eager blind infancy through the productive and procreative years into a senescence that, by the laws of biological instinct as well as the premeditated precepts of stoic virtue, will submit to eternal sleep gratefully?"

And yet so much of his work, his life, is about not submitting gratefully to that eternal sleep, cheating, tricking, denouncing it, protesting it, fixating on it; so much involves the hope for more than our animal walk, an afterlife or, better yet, more life.

In some of his novels he rehearses attitudes of graceful resignation. "If these gnats were not oppressed by death, why should I be?" asks one of his aging gentlemen. Of course, both Updike and the characters he dreamed up *were* oppressed by it, prickled, irritated, tormented, or he would not have written those lines. On some level he liked the idea of a cool or wry resignation; he just did not, for most of his nearly eight decades, inhabit it.

Even some of Updike's last poems, written in the fluorescence of Mass General, seem to be about convincing himself that he is going to die. They ask the question, more than once, of whether he is dying. "Is this an end? I hang, half-healthy, here, and wait to see." The pale, penciled handwriting on the pink paper of that particular poem is so slanted that the words are dangling, literally hanging. He knew, of course, from the medical facts laid out clearly in front of him, that he was dying, but that knowledge may be something that has to be wrestled to the ground.

He did not have time for what Wordsworth called "emotion recollected in tranquillity." Instead, in those arduous last poems, he scrawls through rage, bitterness, bile, jealousy of the living; he works through nostalgia, fond slippage into the past, bewilderment. He writes through magical salvation, resurrection. He imagines himself reading his own death: "Endpoint, I thought, would end a chapter in / a book beyond imagining, that got reset / in crisp exotic type a future I / — a miracle!—could read." He is writing his way out of death; he is dreaming his way past or through it.

On their assorted sheets of scrap paper, the penciled writing of the poems is scrunched, lines crushed together, radically slanted, tilted on the page, handwriting gnarled, and impossible to make out, but the labor comes across. He had very little time and a very long way to go. When he wrote to his editor that he was pushing the poems as far as they could go, that was an understatement; the work is unthinkable, compressed. Words are crossed out for better ones, lines added in, sections scratched out, verbs thought and rethought and rethought again. He wrote to his editor: "My first book was poems; it would be nice to end with another."

In the poems, he also seems to be working toward acceptance, toward a broadening out into the cool universe; he is working toward grace. "God save us from ever ending, though billions have. / The world is blanketed by foregone deaths, / small beads of ego, bright with appetite."

Predictably, one of his strategies is comic deflation. The jokes, the interludes of irony, are comforting because they are in a way an extension of his life, an assertion of personality over the unknown. He writes about his lifelong fear of heights, of flying: "I'm safe! Away with travel and abrupt / perspectives! Terra firma is my ground, / my refuge, and my certain destination. / My terrors—the flight through dazzling air, with / the blinding smash, the final black—will be / achieved from thirty inches, on a bed."

The poems burn through the idea of death, with a new heat and crispness; they process it, synthesize it, master it, to the extent that it can be mastered. They take it from every angle. If style could defeat death, Updike would have.

One of the last poems he wrote was a lovely, wishful expression of an accepting stance toward dying, a new, late iteration of stoicism. It is perhaps the most graceful expression of a peaceful death that I can think of:

With what stoic delicacy does
Virginia creeper let go:
the feeblest tug brings down
a sheaf of leaves kite-high,
as if to say, *To live is good*
*but not to live—to be pulled down*
*with scarce a ripping sound,*
*still flourishing, still*
*stretching toward the sun—*
*is good also, all photosynthesis*
*abandoned,* quite quits.

Is he beginning to understand how acceptance might work, or is this something more like a wish or prayer? One can't know, of course. The writer controls words in ways one can't control feelings. But the beauty convinces; the late poems breathe calm.

He wrote in the dedication of *Endpoint:* "For Martha, who asked for one more book." This is a private reference to that moment when he put his head on the typewriter, saying he couldn't do it, and Martha saying, "Just one more book."

———

In *Rabbit at Rest*, as Rabbit lies in the hospital dying, he sees on his son's face "some unaskable question." He "feels sorry about what he did to the kid." But he can't quite put into words what he wants to say. The last conversation is perhaps the feeling that there is something more to say.

Updike himself does not have a "last conversation" with most of his children. He does not try to exhume old hurts or apologize or resolve. He tries to be cheerful, to be lively, to make conversation. He goes for the smooth and amiable surface. As Miranda put it, "Maybe his struggle to stay cheerful was his form of a last conversation."

He does, however, say formal and eloquent goodbyes to each of his grandsons. He talks to them about their various interests, encourages them. "I thought it was going to be a casual visit," Michael remembers. "And he saw them and he had an agenda, and it was about them. He was wheezing and struggling to get air in his lungs, but he turned over in bed to face them. It was the first time he had focused on them in such an intense way."

In *Endpoint*, Updike wrote about seeing each grandson, "politely quizzing them / on their events and prospects, all the while / suppressing, like an acid reflux, the lack / of prospect black and bilious for me."

Unlike most people, Updike never seemed to regard his children and grandchildren as a feint toward immortality. He referred to the knowledge of his DNA going into the future as "cold comfort." One of his characters "looks at the children and says they're sucking the life out of him." And in the Rabbit books, when Rabbit's granddaughter is born, he thinks: "Fortune's hostage, heart's desire, a granddaughter. His. Another nail in his coffin. His."

He had been, according to Michael, "aloof" as a grandfather. He observed the forms, but there was a lack of real involvement, which most of his children felt to varying degrees. "He would buy a silver cup, but he would not invite his grandkids over to his house. When he would come to visit them, it was like slipping out of the house to see a mistress."

The children and grandchildren were always invited to Haven Hill to watch the fireworks on July 4, but they would watch from the beach. If it rained, Michael says, they either watched in the rain or went home. They were not invited to come into the house and watch from the porch.

———

## JANUARY 25

On Sunday afternoon, Miranda and her sons came to see him. It was a clear, frigid day, and there were snowdrifts on the ground. Fourteen-year-old Kai had written a novel called *Crystal.* Updike told him that he had started it and would try to finish it. He said that he admired Kai's inventiveness and that he hadn't had the stamina to write a whole novel at that age.

He talked to Kai's younger brother, Seneca, who was eleven, about his acting gift and a performance of *A Midsummer Night's Dream* he had seen him in, in October, right before he got sick.

This moment with the grandchildren had a certain formality; it was not the warm, effusive rush some grandparents go in for, but it had meaning for Updike's children. "It was kind of magical," Miranda says. "And I am grateful for it." He was talking to each grandchild specifically, and this specificity seems to be what struck his children. He was responding not to the idea of grandchildren but to the boys in front of him; it was like a blessing, or maybe a statement that he had seen them.

Later that evening, Martha managed to move him out of bed and struggled to get him into a wing chair in their upstairs library for a change of scene. Martha, inveterate traveler, was a big believer in changes of scene. In the chair, he suddenly crumpled up. She wasn't sure what was happening. Could it be a stroke? In a panic, she called the hospice nurse, who came and carried up the box of medications that they kept, according to hospice instruction, in their refrigerator. The nurse gave him some morphine under his tongue with an eyedropper, which immediately calmed him. Together, she and Martha got him into her desk chair, wheeled him to bed, and got the oxygen going again.

The nurse showed Martha how to fill the eyedroppers with morphine. Martha was shaking. She said, "What if I make a mistake?" The nurse said, "There are no mistakes."

The nurse told Martha that he might die in the night and she should be prepared for that. Martha had to wake him every two hours to give him morphine. He made it through till dawn. "It was," Martha says, "the most beautiful night."

As they waited for the ambulance to arrive for the fifteen-minute ride to the small hospice in Danvers, Updike said to Martha, "Are you ready for the leap?"

Martha did not want to say that she was or wasn't ready for the leap. Instead, she asked, "Are you?"

He said, "Yes!"

"I am too," she said. "And so is God."

He'd said yes so loudly, she was surprised.

———

Updike once said that finishing *Rabbit at Rest* was like a kind of death. In the Rabbit books, Rabbit's son is with him when he dies. Nelson is undone at his father's death, demanding that he not die. Rabbit feels some sense of obligation to tell him something. He says, "All I can tell you is, it isn't so bad." He thinks he should say more, but then he doesn't say more. The book ends, "But enough. Maybe. Enough."

In 1990, Philip Roth wrote to him, "Poor Rabbit. Must he die because you're tired?"

Though, of course, it doesn't end. Updike can't resist *Rabbit Remembered,* a continuation of the story without Rabbit. More Rabbit, without Rabbit.

In fact, it seems Rabbit has a robust afterlife because Updike needed to keep him around. He wrote to his friend Warner Berthoff, a professor at Harvard, that he shouldn't joke about Updike doing another Rabbit book in 2009. He says the Rabbit books brought something out in him that nothing else has.

## JANUARY 26

From very far away, the gray-shingled hospice resembled a house, if your vision was very bad. It had only eight rooms; the institution had an overlay of homey-ness, patchwork quilts laid across hospital-like beds.

The Updikes brought a copy of *The Book of Common Prayer*. Martha packed a big duffel for each of them, as if they were going to be there for months.

The children felt that Martha was still restricting their "alone time" with Updike. They did not feel free to stay as long as they liked or come as much as they wanted.

When David and Elizabeth arrived, Updike thanked them for coming so soon. Elizabeth sat on his bed and rubbed his feet through his white socks. They didn't know what he meant by "soon."

When the Episcopal minister from Updike's church arrived, Elizabeth and David recited the Lord's Prayer with him, as they had in their rooms as children.

Updike once wrote:

> Strange, the extravagance of it all—who needs
> those eighteen-armed black Kalis, those musty saints
> whose bones and bleeding wounds appall good taste,
> those joss sticks, houris, gilded Buddhas, books
> Moroni etched in tedious detail?
> We do; we need more worlds. This one will fail.

## JANUARY 27

At the hospice they had a couch in the room that folded out into a bed, and Martha stayed the night.

In the morning, Martha ducked out to take care of something. Michael and Miranda came in. The priest told them it was very near the end.

Updike wrote a peaceful death for Rabbit: "He is nicely tired. He closes his eyes."

Updike had written a peaceful death before he died. He wrote a peaceful death before he was dying, and he wrote it when he was dying: "To live is good / but not to live—to be pulled down / with scarce a ripping sound, / still flourishing, still / stretching toward the sun— / is good also."

When Martha came back, it seemed to her that there was too much going on in the room.

It seemed to her that the children were doing a lot of crying. The priest was doing a lot of praying. She did not want any more praying or crying, so she said, "Clear the room please. I want everyone out."

Michael and Miranda did not want to wait outside, but they waited outside.

Martha read from *The Book of Common Prayer* and talked to him. She had never seen anyone die. He was taking huge loud breaths. She held him and talked to him. His breathing quieted.

Afterward, she went out and got Michael and Miranda and took their hands and brought them in to see their father, an ending so completely in the penumbra of his oeuvre that one can only think: How would Updike write it?

——

In planning his funeral, Updike had said that he wanted a passage from the end of "Pigeon Feathers" to be read aloud. It had not been included in the planned service, so the priest wove it into his own eulogy. The boy is gazing at the dead pigeons' feathers: "He was robed in this certainty: that the God who had lavished such craft upon these worthless birds would not destroy His whole Creation by refusing to let David live forever."

# Dylan Thomas

## NOVEMBER 8, 1953

Dylan Thomas was lying in a coma under an oxygen tent in St. Vincent's Hospital. He had been lying there, unshaven, for three days. The precise cause of the coma was obscure, though he had been heard making the extravagant claim that he had eighteen whiskeys at the White Horse Tavern the night before he collapsed.

It was a bright, cold day. Half of literary New York was gathered outside his room, as if they were still at one of the roving drinks parties that sprang up spontaneously around him.

There was intense competitive jostling about who was closest to him and who was representing his interests. As his wife, Caitlin, put it, "It was like a super melodramatic spy story . . . with all the characters suspecting each other of the vilest motives."

His visitors stood in the hallway, gazing at him through a glass partition. Caitlin, who had always resented the way Thomas was the center of attention, may have been the only one who noticed that even in this situation he had an audience.

Before he was taken to the hospital, Thomas had been staying at the Chelsea Hotel. He was in the middle of a lecture tour. His unnaturally devoted biographer, John Malcolm Brinnin (unnaturally devoted in that he would come into Thomas's hotel room and find him curled up in the fetal position, nude, and would cover him with blankets and turn off the light), had set up a busy schedule of readings.

Thomas was a spectacular reader. At one lecture at the Kaufman Auditorium, with an audience of over a thousand people, the small, plump, rumpled poet stood at the lectern and took out a sheaf of handwritten pages on which he had copied poems. A single shaft of light fell against the blue curtains. His words poured into the velvety darkness: "And death shall have no do-min-i-on." His voice was so rich, so expansive, so majestic, so perfectly enunciated, that one could forgive anyone anything for that voice. Afterward, the audience was wild with applause, young women standing and screaming.

Dylan Thomas had burst into public at nineteen with his first lush poems, many of which, like "And Death Shall Have No Dominion," were preoccupied with death. He wooed readers with the heat of romanticism, the ripe lyricism of an earlier tradition. The literary world, accustomed to the brainy coolness of modernism, to Eliot and Auden, was immediately in thrall to his talent. His friend the poet Elizabeth Bishop said,

162

"Dylan made most of our contemporaries seem small and disgustingly self-seeking and cautious and hypocritical and cold." His reputation for self-destruction, for alcoholism, for erratic behavior, for publicly conducted adultery, and for overall messiness only enhanced his legend and raised his poetry, which was sometimes obscure, to a more beguiling, almost sensual plane. In America, the adulation was magnified, unmanageable. Caitlin wrote later in a letter to a friend, "Nobody needed encouragement less, and he was drowned in it."

For him, the tidal admiration was thrilling, terrifying, alienating; he loved and hated it, felt on some level it was dangerous to him. Elizabeth Hardwick, who was married to Thomas's friend Robert Lowell, put it this way: "Dylan Thomas was loved and respected abroad, but he was literally *adored* in America. Adored, too, with a queer note of fantasy, with a baffled extravagance that went beyond his superb accomplishments as a poet, his wit, amazing and delightful at all times, his immense abilities on the public platform. . . . He was also, and perhaps this was more important to some of his admirers, doomed, damned, whatever you will, undeniably suffering and living in the extremest reaches of experience. . . . Here, at last, was a poet in the grand, romantic style, a wild and inspired spirit not built for comfortable ways."

This was his fourth American tour. The others had carried him across the country, to Boston, Chicago, Colorado, Utah, California. Thomas wrote of one of these tours: "I buried my head in the sands of America: flew over America like a damp, ranting bird; boomed and fiddled while home was burning;

carried with me, all the time, my unfinished letters, my dying explanations and self-accusations. . . ." As this damp, ranting bird made his way across the country, he was feted, and invited to parties, and invited to stay, and the trips were overwhelming, flattering, draining, exhilarating, lonely, addictive. He described himself as being "loudly lost for months." He described himself as "peddling and bawling to adolescents the romantic agonies of the dead." But now he was done with the peddling and bawling. The only sound in the room was the beep of the machines and the faint hiss of the oxygen.

Outside his room, the crowd made dinner plans. People left and arrived in small clumps of twos and threes. The hospital switchboard was barraged with calls. And this was just the beginning. Friends, girlfriends, ex-girlfriends, acquaintances, patrons, poets, critics, and biographers would try to read this coma like one of his denser and more incomprehensible poems. Did Thomas know he was going to die on this trip? Did he drink himself to death? Did someone botch his medical care or fail to take care of him? Did an irresponsible American cohort lead him into a spiral of even more excessive behavior for their own morally suspect reasons? Was it suicide or was it an accident?

———

When Thomas boarded the plane to New York, Caitlin half-thought the unthinkable: that the two of them were splitting up. Their marriage had deteriorated to such an extent that there was certainly in the air when he left the *question* of their

splitting up. They fought bitterly and frequently, and sometimes, after hours in the pub, these fights degenerated into hitting, and it wasn't only, or even largely, Thomas doing the
hitting. There was also hair-pulling, kicking, and plate-
throwing. Caitlin was spirited, prickly, angry, narcissistic; she
did not take well to the inflated ego of her husband, to his
fame, to his perpetual poverty, or even to his irresistible, buoyant charisma at a pub. In photographs, the early smiling ones,
in cable sweaters at the beach, they emanate a tumbling domestic peace, and in the later ones, fatter, sadder, they look like
brother and sister.

Over the last, unhappy years of their marriage, Thomas had
many opportunities to leave. He had seduced other women and
entertained fantasies, at least, about what would undoubtedly
be an easier life with one of them, but he hadn't left.

Perhaps the most serious of these flings was the one he had,
three years earlier, with Pearl Kazin, an editor at *Harper's Ba-
zaar* and sister of the critic Alfred Kazin. She had dark hair
with bangs, an appealing face, a girlish, disheveled, elfin mien.
She was a more substantive person than most of the other
women who surrounded him. He wrote to her once, "There
isn't any future for us; hold me now, in the long undying present, and let me hold you. Oh but London is a beast. Sticky or
grey or both. After eleven at night, dodo dead. I drift discon-
solate through the dead streets, putting off and off my clean,
high, remote and broken room. Would to God that you were
allowed to stay here with me; then the room would be an enormous field, shadowed, full of flowers and running brooks and

bottoms and bottles, where, till the first fissionary gleam, we'd lie close, happy, and half die."

Their time together was fraught with long silences and fevered letters. At one point, she was supposed to meet him in London, but he couldn't see her. In the background he was trying desperately to preserve his marriage and mollify Caitlin, who had heard of the affair. But he continued to write gorgeously to Pearl about the hypothetical plane, the impossible space in which the two of them could continue to meet and conduct their affair. "Oh what a sniveling note to you, my darling, when I could write two War & Peaces. Believe in me. I'm nasty, but I adore you, I wouldn't hurt you. Nothing is impossible for us: it can't be. And out of everything we'll make, somehow, some happiness together again & again & again till the end of whatever."

He continued to write—even from Persia, where he was working on a film script—to Pearl about how much he loved her, and he continued to invoke one day, one night, one moment, they might have together, but he stopped writing about the relationship in practical terms. The fantasy of a life together had passed, though they would continue to meet on his American tours.

The truth is, he didn't seem capable of leaving Caitlin. In which case, what can one do? How does one leave without leaving? Anyone who has lived through the unraveling of a marriage knows that there comes a certain point when death does not seem like an unsensible solution. His state of mind in the days leading up to his coma was hugely affected by his vast, unmanageable anxiety about his marriage. His escape to America was at best temporary. Even he, connoisseur and visionary of the temporary escape, would have known that.

From the beginning, the Thomases' love affair had a desperate quality; it was one of those romantic connections largely fueled by frenzies and fears, largely distinguished by a mad and urgent clinging. Thomas's letters to Caitlin, even at the happiest, most balanced point in their marriage, can only be described as hysterical. He writes, "My dear my dear my dear Caitlin my love I love you; even writing, from a universe and a star and ten thousand miles away, the name, your name, CAITLIN, just makes me love you, not more, because that is impossible, darling, I have always loved you more every day since I first saw you looking silly and golden and much much too good forever for me . . . no, not more, but deeper, oh my sweetheart I love you and love me dear Cat because we are the same, we are the same, we are the one thing, the constant thing, oh dear dear Cat." There is here and elsewhere a fearful, babyish, needy attachment that reveals itself in sharp contrast to his highly articulate and ebulliently controlled letters to nearly everyone else.

Right before Thomas left London, a manager at Lloyds Bank had sent him the following note: "Dear Sir, I write to advise you that as the balance of your account at the close of business today is overdrawn £1.3.2d (one pound, three shillings, and two pence) I regret I have had to return your cheque of £15 payable to self with the answer 'Return to Drawer.' Yours Faithfully, R. Larmour."

A friend remembers a last glance through the window when Thomas boarded the bus at the airport terminal on the final trip to America: Thomas was giving him a thumbs-down sign. By the time he settled into his seat on Pan Am flight 071, Thomas was panicking. Of course, many high-strung people panic on planes; if your life is at all fragile, airplane travel is one of those moments when you feel that fragility most acutely; any lack of structure, of solidity, any sense of the bottom falling out, makes itself felt as the plane rises into the air. But Thomas's panic on the plane was specifically about dying.

He was very precise about that last plane ride: "When I was waiting for the plane this time in London, I found I was drinking in a mad hurry . . . like a fool, good God, one after another whisky, and there was no hurry at all. . . . I had all the time in the world to wait, but I was drinking as though there wasn't much time left for me. . . . I felt as though something in me wanted to explode, it was just as though I were going to burst. I got on the plane and watched my watch, got drunk and stayed frightened all the way here . . . really only a little booze . . . mostly frightened and sick with the thought of death."

At this point, the poet was in his late thirties. No one would deny that he was a little worse for the wear, but he was not suffering from a terminal illness; he was not, in any detectable way, dying. Caitlin said later, "When I last saw him before he went to New York, Dylan seemed tired, but no worse than that . . . he was always complaining about his health, gout, asthma, or other chest infections, but was a much stronger man than anyone ever suspected." Why, then, is he frightened and sick with the thought of death? When he said goodbye to his mother, Florence, he went back to the door three times to kiss her. Rollie McKenna, a photographer who took sad, haunted pictures of him in Wales and later in New York, said that before he left he made the tours of his friends in London and said goodbye as if for the last time. This may be the poetic license of hindsight on McKenna's part, but there is no doubt that on that plane ride to New York Thomas was more than usually afraid of death, and he was afraid of the thing in him that was drawn to death: "something in me wanted to explode."

Once, in happier times, Thomas mimed a clownish suicide for the amusement of his guests. In July of 1951, after lunch, Thomas was sitting on the deck at home, in the boathouse in Laugharne, in the sun, overlooking the sparkling water. The dishes lay strewn across the table. John Malcolm Brinnin was practicing a formal speech he was preparing to give on the radio on the immortal poetry of Dylan Thomas. Afterward, Thomas pretended to hurl himself off the deck and said, "Randy-Dandy Curly-Girly Poet Leaps into Sea from Overdose of Praise."

In the years before he died, Thomas rehearsed his death in jokes. On his second American tour, he wrote a postcard to a friend: "Caitlin and I are buried in the Tuzigoot stone on the other side of the card. We were killed in action, Manhattan island, spring, 1952, in a gallant battle against American Generosity. An American called Double Rye shot Caitlin to death. I was scalped by a Bourbon. Posthumous love to you." There is an eerie clairvoyance here, as he would, in a sense, be scalped by a Bourbon not long afterward, but it is a clairvoyance mingled with the power of humor, the willful, playful, temporary, in the end completely illusory control that language gives over life.

——

## OCTOBER 20

Thomas arrived at Idlewild Airport that last time, sober and unstrung. With his curly, unkempt hair, he looked like a little boy, puffy, awkward. He looked, as someone once observed, like an unmade bed. His current mistress, Liz Reitell, was there to collect him. From the outside, they made an unlikely couple. She was tall, striking, with dark wavy hair, dark-red lips, somehow evoking a movie star from an earlier era.

She was the latest in a string of mistresses, some casual and some not so casual. Women adored him. As the gimlet-eyed Hardwick observed, "So powerful and beguiling was his image—the image of a self-destroying, dying young poet of genius—that he aroused the most sacrificial longings in women. He had lost his looks, he was disorganized to a degree beyond belief, he had a wife and children in genuine need, and yet young ladies *felt* they had fallen in love with him. They fought over him; they nursed him while he retched and suffered and had delirium; they stayed up all night with him and yet went to their jobs the next morning. One girl bought cowboy suits for his children. Enormous mental, moral and physical adjustments were necessary to those who would be the companions of this restless, frantic man. The girls were up to it—it was not a hardship, but a privilege."

As the couple made their way through the airport, Thomas wanted to stop for a drink in the airport lounge, but there were workers picketing, and Liz refused to cross the line, so they took a taxi into the city. He was upset—possibly unduly upset—when they arrived at the Chelsea Hotel and he was not given his usual light room in the front, with a wrought-iron terrace; instead, he was given a smaller, darker, altogether lesser and dingier one in the back. This slight seems to have held some special meaning to him. The world was not treating him as it should; he was being cast aside.

The next morning he was feeling better, and they took a long walk to the West Village. At one point, he and Liz paused on the street to look at a movie poster of *Houdini*. Thomas said that maybe one day he would write a story about Houdini. Houdini the wily escape artist. He'd been interested in Houdini for a long time. Thomas was feeling good, feeling a little bit expansive, on that walk through the brownstone-lined cobblestone streets.

## OCTOBER 27

It was his birthday, and his birthday was troubling him. This was nothing new. His birthdays always troubled him, but this year his birthday was troubling him more. He was turning thirty-nine. Some friends had arranged a birthday party for him in their house in the Village, but he didn't eat anything or talk to anyone. After half an hour he told his host he was feeling too sick to stay, and his host drove him and Liz back to the hotel. As usual, this sickness was something more than physical sickness. He sprawled across the bed and said to Liz, "What a filthy, undignified creature I am."

Approaching another birthday two years earlier, he began to compose "Poem on His Birthday." He described the poem this way: "He looks back at his times: his loves, his hates, all he has seen, and sees the logical process of death in every thing he has been and done. His death lurks for him, and for all, in the next lunatic war. And, still singing, still praising the radiant earth, still loving, though remotely, the animal creation also gladly pursuing their inevitable and grievous ends, he goes towards his. Why should he praise God and the beauty of the world, as he moves to horrible death?" One can only imagine what it was like to live in all the tangle of contradiction here: "*gladly* pursuing this inevitable and grievous end"? Why would a healthy man in his mid-thirties be brooding about death? Why was death lurking in everything he had been and done?

When Thomas was in his late twenties, the war had collided with his obsession with death; it brought the fear closer, gave it shape. Before he was rejected by the army, he was afraid—"my one-and-only body I will not give"—and afterward the bombs haunted him. He described walking to the BBC to talk about a job in the summer of 1940 and then stepping out into a raid. It astonished him that the city was carrying on as usual: "White-faced taxis still trembling through the streets, though, & buses going, & even people being shaved." During another

172

raid, he hid under a table. "Are you frightened these nights?" he wrote to a friend. "When I wake up out of burning birdman dreams—they were frying aviators one night in a huge frying pan: it sounds whimsical now, it was appalling then—and hear the sound of bombs & gunfire only a little way away, I'm so relieved I could laugh or cry."

In the days after his birthday, he was restless and miserable. He lay in his bed in the Chelsea Hotel, complaining. He wanted to go out and buy deli meat for dinner, so he and Liz went out and bought meat, and then when they got back to his room he wouldn't eat it. He distressed Liz by referring to Caitlin as his "widow." With someone so prone to self-dramatization, was it hard to tell how much of this was theater? Could this have seemed simply a new iteration of his Catholic boy's guilt? Could he have wanted his mistress to see his betrayal of his wife in vivid terms so she would feel as bad as he did? Still, it was a powerful thing to say, calling his wife his widow. It was, if nothing else, the trying on of an idea.

It is too simple to say that Dylan Thomas either did or didn't drink himself into the coma. But there are other, smaller, more manageable questions that come to mind. How conscious was Thomas of his faltering health? Did he know that his drinking was wreaking a slow havoc on his body? Did he know that his liver was engorged and fatty? He clearly did not like doctors and avoided them. During these weeks he allowed a handsome and fashionable doctor Liz knew, Milton Feltenstein, to come and inject him with cortisone and consult on his gout and gastritis, but in general he didn't trust doctors.

173

On the cover of his last checkbook, he had scrawled a list of medications for his various ailments: "For nose, Fenox (Boots), chest, codeine soluble, Takazyma (P. Davies) acidity, calomel (liver)."

In 1946, he had been concerned enough about his health to admit himself to a hospital for "drinking obsessions." He had told the doctors at St. Stephen's that he couldn't sleep without drinking. His drinking did not pass unnoticed in his family; before his father died, he often berated his son about it. D. J. Thomas, a schoolteacher, frustrated writer, great reader aloud of Shakespeare, also had a problem with drinking. Over the years, he had forced himself to slow down. Not to stop, but to slow down. He liked to tell his son that if he kept drinking at the rate he was drinking, he wouldn't live past forty.

By September of 1952, Thomas was having blackouts. He fell down a flight of stairs and got a black eye. He fainted in the cinema. He broke his ribs. He broke his arm. He fell asleep drunk and woke up only when a cigarette was burning his hand. He lost his straightforward, physical attachment to life in these moments, and that alarmed him. None of these events on their own signaled that he was dying, but they would have been signals of ill health, warnings perhaps, of the precariousness of his way of life, little flares and flashes of oblivion. In higher spirits, Thomas liked to joke about his many lives: "Life No. 13: promiscuity, booze, colored shirts, too much talk, too little work." However, his doctor in Swansea, where he lived, warned him that if he didn't curb his drinking significantly, one of these episodes would be less than temporary. Is that the kind of warning one truly takes on board? Maybe not. But on some level he must have heard it. Life No. 13 was taking its toll.

In response to a woman friend and patron, Princess Caetani, who wrote a concerned letter about his drinking in January of 1950, Thomas wrote the following: "Yes, I think I'm frightened of drink, too. But it is not so bad as perhaps, you think: the fear, I mean. It is only frightening when I am whirlingly perplexed, when my ordinary troubles are magnified into monsters and I fall weak down before them, when I do not know what to do or where to turn." One imagines this letter may not have been as reassuring as he intended.

———

In the last few weeks of October he was feeling sick, and, more than sick, he was irrationally afraid of this sickness. He broke down one night and told Liz he didn't know if he could go on. Dr. Feltenstein urged him to rest. But he continued to push himself. He had a bronchial infection, which may have been blossoming into a full-scale pneumonia. He was vomiting blood during a rehearsal for the stage adaptation of *Under Milk Wood*; he had written it as a radio play about the inner life of the inhabitants of a Welsh fishing village called Llareggub, which was "bugger all" spelled backward. As he put it, the play was "gay & sad and sentimental and a bit barmy."

John Brinnin offers this unpromising and slightly overwrought description of Thomas's appearance at that rehearsal: "He was liver-white, his lips loose and twisted, his eyes dulled, gelid, and sunk into his head." That same night, Liz Reitell tried to get him to stay in his room at the Chelsea Hotel. "I didn't want to 'reform' Dylan," she would explain. "I wanted to save his life." Whatever her other virtues, however, she was not the most effective nurse. He invited people to his small room for whiskey and beers. He sat in bed and drank with them, still pushing himself.

Thomas had always had a very idiosyncratic relation to the idea of health. He harbored many romantic mythologies about the frailty of his constitution, and one of them centered on the idea that he had consumption. Even when he was a sturdy young man, his sense of theater demanded that he have a poet's constitution, and for some reason he had always held Keats as a point of reference. As a child, he had told his mother he would be better than Keats, and friends remember him proudly showing a bit of blood in his handkerchief, saying, "See, consumption!" One of his friends observed that when he coughed he was like a child drawing attention to his sickness. In fact, Thomas had terrible lungs, but there is no evidence that he ever had tuberculosis. Still, the romantic allure of the disease exerted some influence. Did he want to be sick; did he like the idea of sickness because it answered some need in him? He certainly liked the theater of sickness, the staginess, the attention it brought him, and later the excuses it provided.

Thomas would often invent sicknesses or exaggerate them; it was sometimes a sport to him and sometimes a necessity. He often used sickness and injury as an excuse, to editors, to friends, to patrons. "I have gout, strained back, bronchitis, fits, and a sense of disaster, otherwise very ill," he wrote once, in one of his customary litanies. The complaints slipped and blurred together, because they were not necessarily literal descriptions of his physical state. He was often doing things like not showing up to be best man at a friend's wedding, or not sending in a poem he promised to a magazine, or not showing up at a dinner at which he was being honored. And his abject and ornate and ultimately heartfelt apologies were often filled with colorful and desperate illnesses and ailments. He wrote, for instance, to one of his patrons: "I have been ill for several weeks, in and out of sickbeds in several, and increasingly depressing, furnished London rooms and spiritual orphanages. I caught lots of chills, and they jaundiced me, and I lay snarling at the edge of pleurisy, and I couldn't write or read and I didn't want to think." In general, when he rhapsodized in this way about his health, he seemed to mean something bigger and broader than a single, pinpoint-able physical illness. When he told editors that he was sick with bronchitis and therefore was late on his radio play, or that his whole family had measles and he couldn't finish editing a story, there was an emotional truth to these lies and embellishments: It felt to him that the world was treating him unfairly, that things were too hard for him, and the way he wrote that feeling of desperation into life was to say that he was sick. The sickness was a shorthand, then, a way of talking about his very real sense of constant crisis; it gave a name to the difficulty. Of course, being drunk, and hungover, and generally unhealthy, the physical reality of a slightly broken-down body, with a double chin, a thickened middle, a racking cough, which was not improved by cigarettes, fed into this perception of himself as injured, compromised, and, later, nearly dying. He liked to lie in bed after a particularly long and punishing night out and have Caitlin come and feed him little cubes of bread soaked in milk. This was what his mother used to do, and this was what he liked. The poet found illness a convenient language for his skewed relation to normal life, for his inability at times to function, for his radical abdication of responsibilities. Illness offered, for decades, a comfortable way for him to think about himself. Ever the poet, he pretty much set up camp and lived in the metaphor of being sick.

———

## OCTOBER 31

A private investigator hired by *Time* magazine was following Thomas in the weeks leading up to his death. In what seemed to those around him a doomed and desperate measure, he had begun the process of suing the magazine for libel for saying that he was a drunk and a womanizer, even though he was in fact a drunk and a womanizer and that drinking and womanizing was unusually and extremely well documented. This investigator, then, was following him in these final weeks to try to prove that *Time* had fairly represented his character. So there was a man with a hat and a spiral notebook and pencil lurking in the corners of the bars those last nights, recording for a possible trial the facts and figures of his self-destructive excess. There was—to that extent, at least—the aura of a crime.

On Halloween, Thomas went to a party. His friend John Berryman later said he was barely able to speak, he was so loaded, but they talked a little bit about Ted Roethke's drinking. Then a drunk Thomas went, along with two friends, to the White Horse Tavern at nine. While Thomas was there, the private investigator carefully noted down in pencil, "9:00 p.m. enters W.H.T. . . . drank whiskey and a beer chaser."

Thomas adored the White Horse; it was the closest in New York City he felt to home, with its mahogany bar, its wooden picnic benches, its old-fashioned silhouettes of horses engraved in the windows. Afterward, the three friends moved to another bar on Seventh Avenue. The detective noted: "Describes his impotence. Says how much he loves his wife. Other women and also Caitlin."

And then, at two-thirty in the morning, the private investigator observed Thomas taking Benzedrine pills. Here one wonders at that last notation, piled on the rest. Why did Thomas, after a night of hard drinking, take the extra Benzedrine so he could stay up longer? Why was he pushing himself? Earlier that day the doctor had told him in quite adamant terms to stay in bed. The doctor told him to eat. Thomas was never big on meals. He liked boiled sweets out of a paper bag, Tootsie Rolls, Milky Ways, Baby Ruths, fizzy children's drinks, but the doctor was suggesting meals. The doctor was suggesting sleep. But he was out again, into the city streets, into the night air, into, inevitably, a bar.

Did he know he was going to die? Did the failure of his marriage feel like dying? Was this the only way the poet could dream up of removing himself from the scene? His daughter, Aeronwy, remembers him threatening to kill himself when

Caitlin said she would leave him. And at an earlier point, when Caitlin wrote him a cruel letter after the affair with Pearl, he wrote to her from Persia, "Your letter, as it was meant to, made me want to die. . . . I cannot live without you—you, always—and I have no intention of doing so." On that same trip he wrote, "The sun's shining, & I'm in darkness because I do not know if you will ever love me again. And I'll die if you do not. I mean that. I shall not kill myself: I shall die." This can't, of course, be taken literally; it is precisely the high-blown rhetoric of romantic love that Thomas went in for. But it does express a certain absolutism in his thinking: It lays bare his helpless childlike dependence—Caitlin still cut his nails for him—and his shakiness.

Another anxiety that haunted Thomas during these arduous tours through America was the disconnect between the public poet at the lectern and the private man at home with his notebooks. Thomas was not writing well. He was no longer a poet, he said; he was "a freak user of words." He had written six poems in six years. He observed ruefully to a reporter from *Time*, "It seems as if my faculties for self-criticism have grown more than my talent." And consequently he felt that reading poems in lecture halls put him in a painful position. In a letter to a friend, he wrote, "Endless booming of poems didn't sour or stale words for me, but made me more conscious of my obsessive interest in them and my horror that I would never again be innocent enough to touch and use them." He much preferred reading other people's poems—Yeats, Auden, Roethke, anyone. As he wrote to Princess Caetani, "I do not, now, read any of my poems with much pleasure, because they tell me I should be writing other poems *now*, because they say I should work on poems every day . . . I do not like reading my old poems; because I *am* not working on new poems." Thomas was excellent and creative, however, at wasting time; he wrote once in a letter, "The summer talked itself away."

But in spite of hours whiled away in the pub, in spite of his nearly insatiable need for company, when Thomas was writing, he was fanatical. He wrote draft after draft; when one looks at the scrawlings and scratchings of those drafts, the sheer labor involved in his poems, the huge amount of time and effort expended on a single word, a phrase, is undeniable. He also felt peace and purpose when he was writing. Those rare moments of concentration in his shed at Laugharne were a great salve to him.

But now he felt that his gift was failing, that he had written his best poems. He wrote to an editor the year before, with great shame, "The nagging, savaging, destroying problem, the real reason the book is as yet unwritten, *that* is what you want explained. And how I can write that reason down? *That* is the thing itself: for a whole year I've been able to write nothing, nothing at all but one tangled, sentimental poem." To a poet, this might feel like the end of something more important than life.

It is hard to measure the tangible effects of Thomas's impulse toward self-destruction. There were, however, the vicious swipes of self-hatred. One can chart his self-loathing through his last years. At first it is clownish, playful. He writes of himself to his publisher, "Oh helpless baboon!" But as the years go by, his portraits of himself become more cutting, brutal. He becomes "a little fat man come to make a fool of himself." Sometimes this critical voice is light, teasing, but increasingly it is sharp. He imagines Pearl Kazin walking away from their affair, thinking, "'No more of that beer cheapened hoddy-noddy, snoring, paunched, his corn, his sick, his fibs, I'm off to Greece where you know where you are; oh, his sodden bounce, his mis-theatrical-demeanor, the boastful tuppence!'"

Once, he wrote in a letter, "Thank God I don't have to meet myself socially, listen to myself, or except when reluctantly shaving, see that red, blubbery circle, mounted on ballooning body." Very few people have this store of self-contempt: so physical, so visceral. Does he hate his body itself? Toward the end of his life, there is a tone of precise and furious disappointment, of corrosive sourness, that one recognizes in the late journals of suicides like Sylvia Plath or Virginia Woolf—an eye that can see in human flesh only vicious decay.

Thomas's most beloved and widely read poem, "Do Not Go Gentle into That Good Night," which had been published a year earlier, appears to be a protest against death, an ode to heroic resistance, inspired by his father's death. And yet, if you are in the audience at one of these last readings, your experience of the famous poem is different. When you hear him reciting the familiar line, "Rage, rage against the dying of the light," the cadence is so mesmerizing that it seems to be a poem about acceptance; it lulls you into a feeling of goodwill toward the workings of the universe. Its emotional effect is in fact the opposite of the meaning of the words: It is a paean to the natural order. When one hears the last soft, caressing "Do not go gentle" one can't help but be lost in the loveliness of the lines, seduced. When Thomas stands up onstage, incanting it in his unnaturally beautiful voice, "Though wise men at their end know dark is right," it is a lullaby, drained of violence, drained of anger. You can suddenly hear in his voice what you cannot see on the page: This is on some very peculiar level a love song to death.

———

## NOVEMBER 1

Thomas's friend George Reavey ran into him at the White Horse Tavern in the middle of the afternoon. He was with Liz Reitell and a friend of hers, whom Reavey described as a "dopey drunken architect." Reavey did not think much of Reitell or her friends. Thomas said he'd missed a lunch engagement. He was complaining of "a burnt-up feeling inside." George asked him about Caitlin, and he said, "I don't know if I still have a wife." The dopey architect had a copy of a book by the Scottish poet Norman Cameron, who had died in his forties, six months earlier. Reavey said, "Dylan became concerned about people dying so young. One had a feeling he was talking about himself. Reitell then took him off to some party."

The next day George Reavey saw Thomas again at the White Horse Tavern, in the late afternoon. He looked sick. He was complaining that he had fallen on a rosebush the night before and scratched his eyeball. Reitell came and joined them. She implied that the party had been a wild one and there was a lot of jumping off a table. Reavey wrote, "Christ, I thought. Why are they taking him to parties like that? The man can hardly stand on his two feet."

———

## NOVEMBER 3

He had a few beers with his friend the Scottish writer Ruthven Todd and a few other people at the Chelsea Hotel. He was very funny, riffing on a schizoid bar in which one was one's only customer. Then, because bars were closed for Election Day, Todd took him back to his house for more beers.

———

## NOVEMBER 4

At the last minute, Thomas canceled plans to have steamed clams with Todd in an old saloon in Hoboken, saying he wasn't feeling well. He also canceled plans to go see a play called *Take a Giant Step* with a sculptor friend and went back to the hotel after a few cocktails. He slept fitfully through the evening, next to Liz, waking up several times, weeping about his smallest son, towheaded Colm: "Poor little bugger, he doesn't deserve this. Doesn't deserve my wanting to die." Not "my dying." My "wanting to die."

At one point he woke and sat up in bed. He told Liz that he had to go out and have a drink. Liz tried to dissuade him. It was two in the morning. The doctor had told him to rest. He dressed and went out. Liz stayed up in the dark hotel room waiting for him to come back. "Even the cockroaches have teeth," Thomas had said of that room. He finally stumbled in and reported into the shadows: "I've had eighteen straight whiskeys. I think that's the record."

When he woke up in the morning, he wanted air, so they went for a walk. They ended up in the dark woody interior of the White Horse Tavern for a couple of beers. He was supposed to go pick up a dinner jacket from one of his friends' houses, but Liz persuaded him to go back to the Chelsea instead. There he vomited and slept, and vomited and slept. Following the doctor's instructions, she gave him phenobarbital, but he couldn't keep the pill down. The doctor came and gave him a shot of morphine, which was then a fairly common treatment for excessive alcohol consumption, though it may not have been wise given the severity of the problems with his lungs.

"What did he say to you?" Thomas asked Liz afterward. "Did he say I was going to die?"

"No," she said. "He simply said that you will have to accept the fact that you are very ill and you'll have to begin today to do something about it."

That evening, Liz believed he suffered delirium tremens, hallucinating what he called "abstractions"—triangles, squares, and circles. Liz called a friend, a painter, to come over and help her watch him. Thomas said, "Hello, Jack, awful for you to have to do this," but the painter shrugged this off. Thomas continued, "What an undistinguished way to reach one's thirty-ninth year."

A little after midnight, Thomas got worse. His breathing was ragged. His skin was blue. Liz called the doctor again. An ambulance came, and a stretcher bearing Thomas was carried down the stairs with its wrought-iron banister and through the lobby with its black-and-white floor tiles. They brought him to St. Vincent's Hospital on 13th Street and Seventh Avenue at a little after two in the morning. His medical records show that he had suffered "a severe insult to the brain."

At five in the morning, Liz called Ruthven Todd, who hurried to the hospital from his house in the Village. By eight, John Brinnin arrived, having flown in from Boston, and friends, admirers, lovers, poets, publishers, gawkers, began to descend.

The precise origin of Thomas's coma has been the subject of fierce dispute. There is a certain murkiness in the medical records, which has fed the theories and speculations of those who did not accept the events of the evening as a natural outcome of his behavior. One of the doctors who examined him diagnosed him with "direct alcoholic toxicity in brain tissue." But there are people who argue that Thomas didn't succumb to drink. There are people who argue that he was not, at any point in his life, an alcoholic. One critic would claim his "drinking was often more moderate, and more complex, than the legend would have us believe" and that he was not an alcoholic, because "of his periods of abstinence, displays of moderation and his preference for beer over wine and spirits." This loyal and imaginative collection of friends and critics would like to preserve the image of his vitality, of his robust celebration of God's earth; they are invested in his public defiance of death and want him to remain the booming, confident author of "And Death Shall Have No Dominion" and "Do Not Go Gentle into That Good Night." In the service of this image, they prick and prod at the events of the November night in hopes of somehow clearing the poet's name. They seem to believe that if they could somehow prove that his coma was a pure accident or sheer medical malpractice, it would clear him of any responsibility or involvement in his own early death. In supporting their view, many of them have pored over his medical records. A doctor named William Murphy wrote a paper called "Creation and Destruction: Notes on Dylan Thomas," in which he said, "It remains a mystery how so obviously and gravely ill a person, mentally and physically, could have remained outside a hospital." And there are certainly reasonable questions about his treatment in the days leading up to his death. Why did Dr. Feltenstein allow him to walk around in such a wretched physical state, without ordering further tests or taking stronger steps to ensure the rest and abstention he was advocating?

*The Death of Dylan Thomas*, a zealous account by Dr. James Nashold and George Tremlett, put forth the questionable theory that diabetes killed him and that he was, in fact, at the height of his creative powers when he died. (The evidence for this theory includes his mood swings, his depression, his blackouts, and his taste for candy; it dismisses urine tests that are negative for glucose.) There is in some of this ardent biographical conjecture the ambience of a murder scene: "Thomas' death was not as straightforward as the legend suggested. Why was everyone so quick at the time to blame alcohol? Why did they make no allowance for the body's ability to metabolize alcohol? . . . Why were no laboratory tests ordered when Thomas' problems first manifested themselves? Why was the truth concealed from his wife? Whose reputation was being protected by this cover-up? The doctors', the hospital's, Brinnin's or the mysterious mistresses'?" In the final pages of the book, the authors conclude that the poet "was struck down in his prime by a doctor who should have known better." In this same line of interpretation, there are dark insinuations about why it took Liz Reitell so long to get him to the hospital after he was unconscious.

And yet these insinuations and theories seem curiously incidental to the death that was hovering over Thomas. Whether he had diabetes or an engorged liver, whether his system was weakened by alcohol or a complex combination of other conditions, including his pneumonia, he was still defying medical advice and common sense in pushing himself beyond reasonable limits. He knew he was sick, and he continued rather ardently and resourcefully to make himself sicker. If he had not died that week, surely he would have died sometime not long afterward. By the time he arrived in America, he had wished or worried himself into a physical state impossible to sustain. At some point, the poet's morbid and overblown fear of death transformed itself into barreling headlong toward it.

Wild rumors began to spread. The poet had fallen down a flight of stairs. He had been attacked on the street. He had pricked his eye on a rose. *The New York Times* ran a laconic notice: "Dylan Thomas, Welsh poet, was in St. Vincent's Hospital yesterday with a serious brain ailment. Mr. Thomas, who is 39 years old, collapsed late Wednesday night in his quarters at the Hotel Chelsea."

For those who would like to contest the events of Thomas's last conscious night, the eighteen straight whiskeys have taken on a luminous importance. There are hefty biographies that devote pages and pages to the question of whether he drank eight drinks on that last night or eighteen as he boasted. Several of his friends went to the White Horse Tavern to grill the bartenders on how many whiskeys they had served him. They examined the bottle of Old Grand-Dad on his dresser at the hotel to see how many glasses had been consumed. All of this sleuthing springs from an effort to establish Thomas's innocence somehow, to make him a spectator or a victim in the night's murderous events. One of his biographers reasoned, "Why would he go out at all when there was whiskey in his room?" It is as if the answer to the question of whether he had eight whiskeys or eighteen could somehow undo the fact that Thomas had died or could transform him into a moderate, sensible man who did not abuse his body or entertain any ambivalence about continuing on. Even Liz Reitell, who knew he was an alcoholic, made the implausible claim: "He was either sober or semi-sober most of the time that I was with him."

It seems clear, however, that whatever the exact blood alcohol content of Dylan Thomas's last few days, the coma was part of a script that was already being written, as surely as the script for *Under Milk Wood*. It may have been an accident, but it was an accident that was so thoroughly imagined, so thoroughly thought through ahead of time and incorporated into a world-view, so intrinsic to who he was or had become, that one can't view it as totally separate and discrete from the man's life.

If Thomas did not literally have eighteen whiskeys, there was in the claim, in the swagger and excess of it, something true to the magnitude of his thirst. If he was not giving an accurate account of his bar tab, he *was* giving an accurate and realistic account of his need to escape, of the distance he needed to travel to get away, of the urgency of that flight and transport. Take an average evening at any point in Thomas's life: One sees the effort to go on for one more hour, one more drink, one more Benzedrine, one more story, one more joke. Thomas was the kind of man who wanted to stay out because to be at home in bed was to surrender to nothingness. This is one of the reasons for the insomnia from which Thomas suffered: the desire to prolong, to keep going, to stave off a frightening quiet, which is being alone with oneself. Thomas found drinking the best cure for insomnia.

Is this itself the protest? Is this the "rage, rage against the dying of the light"? Five drinks, six drinks, seven, the desperate desire to carry on—is this the force that took Thomas out of his room in the Chelsea Hotel at two-thirty in the morning to go to the bar? Was every night for Thomas a little bit the last night on earth?

His last few weeks were filled with a self-torment that was ratcheted up higher than it had been before. And yet, in all this hurtling toward the White Horse Tavern in a taxi, it is interesting that he was still grasping at happiness—that he was going to have sex with a new woman in these days, that he would seek out more conversation, that he was not finished with pleasure. His words hang over these last days: Celebrate animal creation, though remotely. The interesting thing in these last painful, mad days is how much love there is of life.

In 1945, a younger, unharmed Thomas wrote the beautiful lines, "Time held me green and dying / Though I sang in my chains like the sea." This is from the poem "Fern Hill." For Thomas, one could be young and dying, green and vibrant and still dying. There was no contradiction here: Everyone was dying, everything was dying, and the world was more gorgeous and miraculous because of it. One of his old drinking buddies from Swansea remembers Thomas turning to him in his twenties and saying, "I've got death in me."

———

In many ways, Thomas's approach to longevity or the long haul reveals itself in his approach to money. Take the thousands of dollars he earned from his American tours. He was paid handsomely for readings, for his famous booming voice, for his appearance in a shabby tweed jacket, for his colorful and outrageous behavior at the faculty parties afterward. In fact, the entire point of the American tours was to make enough money to enable him to write quietly in the shed in Laugharne, but the lecture fees vanished like a child's sand castle by the ocean. After Thomas's first tour, John Brinnin hid eight hundred dollars for Caitlin in a purse packed in Thomas's suitcase, because he knew that if Thomas found it he would spend every single penny on the ship before he got home. How did he go through all this money so quickly? At one point, Brinnin noted, Thomas was spending one hundred dollars in a day, not including his hotel. This was fairly impressive in an era when a cocktail at a New York bar cost sixty cents. Traveling across the country, Thomas would sometimes run out of money and Brinnin would have to wire him funds, because all of a sudden Thomas couldn't afford cigarettes or cab fare. Why couldn't he think to wire for money before he literally ran out? Why, at around this same time, couldn't he save a tiny portion of one of his lecture fees for his son's tuition, before the boy was thrown out of school? His attitude was the same at home. He wouldn't pay taxes until the government tracked him down and demanded them. He wrote checks for money he didn't have in his bank account, even after notices that the account was overdrawn. He was in fact earning quite a significant amount of money by that point, but he couldn't hold on to it. One can't help thinking his radical irresponsibility about money says something about his apprehension of time: Life is not scrolling forward for Thomas in the usual way. The day, the hour, the pub he is in, are in some very real sense the end of the world.

There again is the pause on his walk to the West Village with Liz Reitell, when he stopped to look at the poster for *Houdini*. There are the chains, the locked wooden boxes at the bottom of the sea, the miraculous, improbable stunt of escape. Maybe he will write a story about Houdini. Maybe he will write a story. And yet they move on, subsumed into the crowd on the cobblestone streets. Thomas wrote one of his very last letters, a sort of delirious fantasy about himself as Houdini at the bottom of the sea, to Princess Caetani: "Oh, one time the last time will come and I'll never struggle, I'll stay down here forever handcuffed and blindfolded, sliding my woundaround music, my sack trailed in the slime, withal the rest of the self-destroyed escapologists in their cages, drowned in the sorrows they drown and in my piercing own, alone and one with the coarse and cosy damned seahorsey dead, weeping my tons." Is this what Thomas was? A self-destroyed escapologist. There seems no better description. Weeping his tons.

Thomas was not someone who lived easily and naturally with the idea of consequences. Often when he was staying with rich people, he would steal something from them. He would open their closets and put several of their fine cotton shirts in his suitcase, for instance. He would be caught, and he knew he would be caught, but this being caught was so abstract to him—as it took place in the hazy and nebulous future, when you would be called into account for all the things you were called into account for—that it didn't mean anything. As a result, the great poet had a large number of other people's beautiful shirts.

How does one sing in one's chains like the sea? One starts with a lot of drinks. Then a new woman, or two new women, or two new women in the space of a single evening. On one of his last desperate days, Thomas went upstairs at a party in a townhouse on Sutton Place and had sex with the countess who was hosting the party, while his mistress Liz Reitell drank gin and tonics downstairs. This has a quality of fever, of someone determined to squeeze not one life but several out of an evening. This may be how one sings in one's chains like the sea.

His friend Robert Lowell put it this way: "He gave a great feeling of health and unhealth, of someone who was ruining himself. The joy seemed very real and the darkness seemed very real and neither of them seemed to exist without the other."

In some sense what makes people love Thomas is this almost grotesque vitality, the irrepressible, irresistible, sensual celebration he could not help but write. It pulses through his most beloved lines: "The force that through the green fuse drives the flower." There is an almost cartoonish life, an overbrimming energy in his poems that even people who do not in general respond to poetry can appreciate. Why *should* he praise God and the beauty of earth as he moved to horrible death? The protest, the great loud mournful animal cry, the violence, are all there, rolled up with the praise. The beautiful and the life-giving can't be separated from death. "The force that through the green fuse drives the flower / Drives my green age; that blasts the roots of trees / Is my destroyer." It is this paradox, this morbidity mingled with celebration, the great seductive virile power of nature, combined with a constant awareness of its killing that is the essence of Thomas. There is something of this same too muchness in his days. It makes one think of a line he wrote once to a girl he was flirting with: "Perhaps my nature itself is overwritten."

And indeed Thomas's behavior in New York in those last weeks seemed to be setting up the contradiction: How could someone with that much life in him die? The sick man who felt compelled to get out of bed at two-thirty in the morning and go to the bar for more beer, for more conversation, more jokes, how does that man die? Thomas worked through this paradox in his unfinished elegy to his father: "Too proud to die, broken and blind he died." The heartbreak of it, the protest, is putting it all in one line separated by only the comma. In this way he telegraphs the tragic reversal, the intrusion of reality. It doesn't matter how proud he is. He dies anyway. And right beneath it the rhythm of protest: He can't die! He's too proud to die!

As she sat next to his hospital bed, did Liz Reitell think of that poster of Houdini, of the death-defying magician? Now he lay there, his eyes opening every now and then. Did he know she was there? Liz sat there for days, doing the work of watching him die. She may have wondered if she was the right person to be sitting there. There was a telegram from his wife lying on the table next to his bed, and Liz knew she was on her way to New York. Liz had tried to leave him in those last days leading up to the coma—one night she told him to drop her off at her apartment in a cab—but she had failed.

———

## NOVEMBER 7

It was a dark, snowy day. Thomas's wife, Caitlin, arrived at the hospital in a tight black wool dress, her ash-blond hair pinned up in the usual falling-down bun, still the same bloom or radiance people always commented on, the same slightly menacing quality of too muchness. She was a bit drunk, and who could blame her? Knowing Caitlin was on her way, Liz Reitell had tactfully cleared out. When Caitlin saw Brinnin, she called out, "Is the bloody man dead or alive?" What happened next was that Caitlin interfered with Thomas's breathing. Ironically, she was trying to be socially acceptable. She later said, "I thought I had to make some gesture of affection to Dylan, because there they all were, looking at me through that window. I started to try to get closer to him; I wanted to give him a hug, so I sort of rolled on top of him. The nurse came bustling in and pulled me off. 'You'll suffocate him.'" A little while later, Caitlin also lit a cigarette dangerously close to the oxygen tank, which the nurse didn't like much either. She was told that she had to leave.

The next time she visited, Caitlin smashed a crucifix on her way out. She knocked over a statue of the Virgin Mary. She bit an orderly on the hand. To anyone watching, it was as if Thomas's wife was doing his not going gently for him. Some felt the hospital was overreacting: She was taken from there in a straitjacket to River Crest, a sanitarium in Queens.

—

## NOVEMBER 8

John Berryman and Pearl Kazin were at a conference at Bard College. Berryman was shaken by the news of Thomas's condition. He drunkenly recited "Do Not Go Gentle into That Good Night" at a party, and he and Pearl called St. Vincent's repeatedly, trying to get information about Thomas.

That night, they drove back with Ralph Ellison and arrived at the hotel at midnight. Berryman and Pearl went to the hospital and persuaded the nun in charge to let them in. They went into the darkened room and saw him under his oxygen tent.

——

## NOVEMBER 9

At lunchtime, Brinnin stepped out of the room to get a cup of coffee and to talk to some of his friends in the waiting room. John Berryman stayed with Thomas. The tall, nervous, bearded poet from Princeton had been one of the most dedicated hoverers. A few minutes after one, Berryman rushed out in the hall to find Brinnin. "He's dead! He's dead! Where were you?" When Thomas died, Berryman was "the breathing nearest other thing," as he wrote later in a poem, though technically a nurse was nearer. The nurse had been bathing him when he died. She rolled him onto his side and began washing him with a damp cloth, and he stopped breathing. There was no struggle, no gasp for air. Berryman wrote in a letter to a friend, "His body died utterly quiet."

Brinnin and Liz followed Berryman into the room. The nurses were taking down the oxygen tent. Detached from all the machines, holes in his flesh from tubes, the poet lay like a chunky pietà on the starched white sheets. The biographer held his feet in his hands. They were already cold. The postmortem account would read: "obese trunk, puffy face; wavy brown hair on head; moderate frontal baldness; brown eyes; unshaven face . . . all teeth show discoloration—several teeth missing in lower jaw."

In all of his imagining and reimagining of this moment, Dylan Thomas wrote what in another kind of man would be called prayer. He wrote death as comforting; he wrote great billowing consolations, exalting even in the enduring power of the universe, a shared dream of infinite renewal. He wrote, "That the closer I move / To death, one man through his sundered hulks, / The louder the sun blooms / And the tusked, ramshackling sea exults." There is grandeur here and peace. This poem, written four years earlier, ends "As I sail out to die."

In this pretty image of sailing out to die there is an element of the child comforting himself. One thinks of Thomas turning back not once but three times to kiss his mother goodbye the last time he saw her. One thinks of a night when the bombs fell on London during the Blitz, when Thomas lay the wrong way in the bed, with his head under the sheets, with his wife reading calmly, the right way round, the noise crashing around them.

Before Thomas's coma, Caitlin had written him a letter from Wales. This is the letter he knew that she was writing, but it arrived too late for him to read it. If he had recovered, he would have read the words: "I knew you were abysmally weak, drunken, unfaithful and a congenital liar, but it has taken me longer to realize that on top of each one of these unpardonable vices, you are a plain, stingy meany as well. . . . There is, without exception, no wife in the whole of creation treated like I

198

am, and at last it's over for better or worse. And no more slop talk, let's at least cut that out—you may be good at it, but it stinks to high heaven, turn it on one of your new adulators, it always goes down. Whatever you do or say, however foul, always goes down, fuck you."

When she heard about Thomas's death, Elizabeth Bishop wrote to Pearl Kazin, "I think I had expected to hear news like that at any time, but even so it is a bad shock." Indeed, his death was, to many, both a great shock and utterly anticipated. The collision of his vividness, his vitality, with his self-destruction was hard to assimilate; it seemed both impossible and inevitable, and the grief it inspired was intense, confused.

The autopsy report read: "CAUSE OF DEATH: PIAL EDEMA: FATTY LIVER: HYPOSTATIC BRONCHO-PNEUMONIA." The true mystery of Thomas's last days, however, is not the precise medical cause of his coma; it is how the unnatural fear and apprehension of death melts into a craving for it. His long preoccupation with the end, with all the celebrating and singing one can do on the way to that end, his overdeveloped, painful consciousness, always, of that end, is transformed into something almost beautiful. It seems if you are afraid or preoccupied with something for long enough, you begin to develop a feeling toward it not dissimilar to love. This is not a trick of the mind that most healthy people can understand. David Foster Wallace once wrote, in a *Harper's* piece about a cruise ship, a decade before his own suicide: "The word 'despair' is overused and banalized now, but it's a serious word, and I'm using it seriously. It's close to what people call dread or angst, but it's not these things, quite. It's more like wanting to die in order to escape the unbearable sadness of knowing I'm small and weak and selfish and going, without doubt, to die. It's wanting to jump overboard."

In Thomas's wallet, there was a faded clipping from a Welsh local newspaper. It had a photograph of him winning a long-distance race as a child. He had carried it around with him for thirty years. He was a slim, beautiful boy winning a race. Of all the interviews, the awards, the profiles, this is what he kept with him in his wallet, this clean victory, this running and winning, in a time before he was running and not winning.

Several years before his own suicide, John Berryman wrote in a letter to Robert Lowell: "Dylan murdered himself with liquor. Tho' it took years." When he was young and healthy, Thomas had referred to his poems as "statements made on the way to the grave."

One can't help thinking Thomas would have enjoyed the fact that his funeral, in Laugharne, was by no means a solemn or orderly or upright occasion. Drink flowed freely. Fights broke out. Several of his papers were stolen off the battered wooden desk in his writing shed behind the boathouse.

# Maurice Sendak

APRIL 14, 2012

Maurice Sendak had an unusually bad headache. He thought it was the beginning of a migraine and went to bed, but by morning it was so bad that his companion, Lynn Caponera, called an ambulance. The ambulance took him to Danbury Hospital. A blood vessel had broken in his brain. His balance and swallowing had been affected.

———

Maurice had always been obsessed with death. He drew through his obsession, used it. He drew lions that would swallow you; he drew wild things that gnashed their terrible teeth; he drew faceless hooded goblins stealing babies out of a window; he drew fat bakers who'd bake you up in a pie; he drew a nine-year-old pig that promised he would never turn ten. He drew funny, charming, cheerful, haunting near-deaths. He drew narrow escapes, popping up, resurrection.

He knew what it was like to be so depressed that dying did not seem crazy or outlandish or remote. He had a kind of intimacy with death, with the idea of it, anyway.

Even as a tiny child in Brooklyn, Maurice was unusually alert to the prospect of dying. He was floored by every childhood sickness—measles, scarlet fever, double pneumonia. "My parents were not discreet," he said. "They always thought I was going to die." He laid out the toy soldiers on the blankets of his sickbed. He watched other children play through the window.

One day his grandmother, who had emigrated from the shtetls outside Warsaw, dressed him in a white suit, white shirt, white tights, white shoes, and took him out to the stoop to sit with her. The idea was that the angel of death would pass over them and think that he was already an angel and there was no need to snatch him from his family.

During one illness Maurice had as a toddler, his mother found him clawing a photo of his grandfather that hung above the bed; he was speaking Yiddish, even though he only knew English. She thought a dybbuk was trying to claim him from beyond the grave, so she tore up the photograph. She said she burned it, but years later Maurice found the torn-up pieces in a Ziploc bag among her possessions. He had a restorer put it back together and he kept it in his house, this grandfather calling him to the grave.

The general message from his family seemed to be that he should be grateful to be alive, that his continued existence involved some aspect of luck that should not, if he was smart, be pushed. When he was very small, his parents told him that when his mother was pregnant they went to the pharmacy and bought all kinds of toxic substances to induce a miscarriage, and his father tried pushing her off a ladder. They hadn't wanted a third child. Why would they tell a tiny child this? As a famous artist, later in life, he brushed the question off in an interview, as though it wasn't in fact a big deal—they were harried immigrants, they didn't need another mouth to feed, though surely something deeper was etched into his sense of himself. He was unwanted, unwelcome, somehow meant to die, meant to be carried off. He said once, "I felt certain my mother did not like me."

———

Maurice had bought the house next door to his in Ridgefield, Connecticut, and he invited young illustrators to come and stay there, as a kind of artists' colony. One of these illustrators, Aaron, had a pair of track pants that Maurice particularly liked. Aaron had given them to Maurice, and Maurice wore them around the house; then he wore them in the hospital. Somehow the hospital laundry lost Aaron's track pants, and Maurice was upset. Lynn Caponera, who spent every night at Danbury Hospital with Maurice, went out to buy him new track pants, this being something she could fix, but somehow they couldn't quite replace Aaron's track pants.

———

There is a formal photograph of his dumpling-shaped mother, her wavy hair chin length, with her three wary children, the wariest of all being baby Maurice, who is dressed in a white bonnet and appears from his scowl to already be seeing some pretty wild things. She is looking at the camera as if it might at any moment leap out and attack her. Theirs was not a happy or relaxing home. Sadie Sendak was often furious. She had trouble with warmth. The siblings turned to one another, sometimes sleeping together like kittens, three in a bed. Maurice, who struggled in public interviews to be generous to his mother, said that she should never have had children, and distant, absent, prickly, punishing mothers would be a big obsession of his books.

His mother's anger was a large part of his childhood, her love for her children suffused with rage and resentment. In addition to the usual immigrant stress, she suffered from serious clinical depression. Once, when Maurice was little, a friend was over, and his mother was furiously fuming and stomping through the house. The friend said, "Who is that?" and Maurice, embarrassed, said, "Oh, we had to hire someone."

The literary critic Stephen Greenblatt once wrote about Sendak's books: "Love often takes the form of menace, and safe havens are reached, if they are reached at all, only after terrifying adventures."

All his life Maurice bristled at the idea of childhood innocence and at those who thought his books were offending or challenging it. In a comic Art Spiegelman did in *The New Yorker* of a conversation they had in the woods, Maurice says: "People say,

'Oh, Mr. Sendak. I wish I were in touch with my childhood self, like you!' As if it were all quaint and succulent, like Peter Pan. Childhood is cannibals and psychotics vomiting in your mouth! . . . In reality, childhood is deep and rich. . . . I remember my *own* childhood vividly. . . . I knew terrible things . . . but I knew I mustn't let adults *know* I knew . . . it would scare them."

Maurice liked to tell the story of the daughter of a friend who was at school near the World Trade Center when the towers fell. She told her father that she saw butterflies on the building as the towers collapsed. Later she admitted that they weren't butterflies, they were people jumping, but she didn't want to upset her father by letting him know that she knew. Children protect their parents, which is the funny part of childhood that slips away from us, the awful knowledge it contains.

The received wisdom is that it is not good to scare kids, but Sendak's belief was that kids are already scared, that what they crave is seeing their anxieties thrillingly laid out. Much of Sendak's work, then, exists between play and terror, that infinitely intriguing, purely fantastical place where you are joked out of your most serious fears. But those fears are also entertained on the most serious and high level in Sendak's books; they are not dismissed but reveled in, romped through.

Sendak liked to talk about artists who "hid" things in their art—composers like Schubert, for instance. This was a model he applied to himself, the idea of hiding something big and grave in a modest form. He brought the seriousness of a great artist to what seemed to some like a small, humble, or limited

207

form, and in it he expressed himself entirely. He came of age as an artist when abstract expressionism was the rage, and his unfashionably naturalistic work would have been scoffed at in the art world, but in the narrow field of children's books, he brought his fierceness and spirit and gift to bear on his illustrations. He "hid" many things in his books: rage, terror, death, abandonment, loss, sex, guilt. His themes were the big ambitious themes of all art, but they were hidden in a world of wild things and sailboats and shaggy dogs.

The fantasy of smuggling himself into his art also perhaps owes something to being gay in an era that would not easily accept homosexuality. He hid his sexual preference from his parents. He kept it from readers and reviewers for far longer than seemed necessary. He came out explicitly in public, at the encouragement of his very close friend, the playwright Tony Kushner, in an interview in *The New York Times* when he was eighty. The interviewer asked him if there was anything he had never said in an interview, and he said, "Well, that I'm gay." Toward the end of Sendak's life, a young interviewer asked him when he had stopped beating himself up for being gay, and he said he never did; the sense of something shameful, or secret, or socially unacceptable stayed with him as an artist even after he came out, even in his eighties.

Children's books had very little prestige when he was starting out. He jokes about going to a cocktail party and a man asking him what he did. "I am a children's book illustrator," he replied. And the man, looking over his shoulder, said, "Oh, well, I am sure my wife would love to talk to you."

Even after *Where the Wild Things Are* came out and he achieved the kind of overwhelming, life-altering fame usually reserved for movie stars, he did not rest or stop working crazy hours or feel appreciated. He still felt like he was laboring in a largely hostile and uncomprehending world.

All his life Maurice felt a particular affinity for artists and writers who were misunderstood, unappreciated, uncelebrated. He had a great passion for the story of Keats, or Melville, or Blake, or anyone who was not recognized in their time. This particular passionate identification was ironic, of course, as few artists are as celebrated, famous, feted, and beloved in their times as Sendak was. He was not exactly laboring in obscurity. But there was something in the experience of dying unknown that he recognized: He may have felt famous but not seen.

———

In the early sixties, Maurice did a watercolor of the man who would be his partner of fifty years, Dr. Eugene Glynn; he called the painting *Landscape with Gene*. The landscape is a pale, watery blue green, the plants lushly delicate, gentle, almost as if you could swim through them. Gene sunbathes on a chaise longue in a striped button-down shirt and shorts, long legs bent gracefully, deeply lost in a book. The scene exudes warmth, affection, a fertile peace.

Gene was tall, imposing, smart, opinionated, erudite, especially about art, in a way that Maurice, who never went to college, particularly admired. He was also a psychoanalyst who worked with adolescents. Like Maurice, he had a profoundly difficult childhood—his father had been shot and killed—and was driven by the idea of repairing early wounds, fixing childhood pain.

Also very early on, Maurice did a portrait of him in a charcoal suit—angled, opaque, uncomfortable, slightly rumpled, with a romantic masculine aura of a secret unhappiness or dark past.

For most of their decades-long relationship, Gene went to work in the city and came up on weekends, so they lived together but not every day of the week. In the later decades, Gene would go to Europe with friends over the summer and Maurice would stay home.

Maurice had a flair for compartments. When he finally introduced Tony Kushner to Gene, it was a big deal; the mixing and mingling of worlds did not come easily or naturally to him, and he had many passionate friendships that he kept entirely separate.

At one point, Maurice became enchanted with a monastery in upstate New York where the monks raised German shepherds. He visited over the years and bought a farm near it. He had the idea he might escape there. He never brought Gene to the farm. Another compartment in a life of compartments.

And yet the two of them were deeply linked. Maurice sketched a cartoon at the bottom of a letter to someone else that was a forecast of his weekend. A tiny Maurice is sitting in the boxy house, gazing out the window, the trees curling behind him like smoke, complaining that he can't work. Outside, the shirtless caretaker has broken a planter, and says that he's worried about Gene and Maurice's reaction, and Gene, bearded, holds up his hand and runs after the three dogs, shouting their names. Here the distracting unrest of domestic life is sweet; the dashed-off cartoon of household annoyances exudes tenderness.

———

In the hospital, Maurice put on a good front so the few very close friends who came to see him wouldn't worry. He was doing physical therapy. He was being a very good patient— perhaps too good a patient, Lynn thought, as he was letting things go instead of complaining, which was unlike him. Lynn advocated for him, but his passive acceptance of hospital life did not seem to bode well.

On the phone, she would tell friends about his progress, as if he were getting better slowly.

———

If one ever had a fantasy of a mother who would be eternally available, hovering protectively in the background, baking cakes, making lunch, driving you places, buying clothes, dispensing an unconditional and undemanding love, Lynn Caponera did a fairly good job of approximating that role. In general this is not something you can pay for, not a service you can buy, but if you are very lucky or unusually gifted in human relations, it is something you can stumble into. It is maybe a testament to the sheer magnificent force of Maurice's imagination that he did not create only the superbly benign mother who leaves Max a hot dinner after their fight in *Where the Wild Things Are* but also conjured Lynn into his own exuberant, fretful life.

For most of her life, Lynn lived with Maurice and took care of him. On rare occasions when Lynn went out to dinner, Maurice told her that if she stayed out past eleven he would get worried, and he would get sick, and his heart would beat too fast, and he would have trouble breathing. In fact, if she came home a little late, at, say, eleven-twenty, she would find him taking labored breaths. Other people would say that he was manipulating her, but she would say, "No, he really is sick. It makes him sick if I am out too late."

Maurice wanted Lynn to do things for him: If he needed a nurse, it had to be Lynn; if someone was going to pick up a pair of pants for him in several sizes and then return the ones he didn't want to the store, or make him a sandwich, it had to be Lynn. Sometimes other people would point out the irrationality of this, but in his mind it had to be Lynn. The dependence was absolute, draining, flattering, consuming; the quasi-maternal care demanded of her was magnificent in scope. The particular quality and seductiveness of the need will be recognizable to mothers of very small children, most of whom won't rise to it.

When Lynn first wandered over as an eleven-year-old with pretty sky-blue eyes, from her family's house down the road, her brother, Peter, was already working in Maurice's house as a kind of handyman and caretaker. He came with the house, as everyone put it. One day Lynn was helping with the weeding. Her mind drifted and she did a shoddy job, and Maurice told her that she should always do her job, whatever it was, as well as she could.

She would sometimes come over and look after the puppies he was breeding. They would be out on the porch, and Maurice wanted someone to pay attention to them and watch over them. Neither Maurice, a children's book illustrator, or Gene, an adolescent psychiatrist, had much experience actually taking care of children, so for lunch they would give her whatever she wanted. She would wolf down chocolate bars and Tab, and later in the afternoon she would feel sick.

Maurice and Gene talked to her about art and books. She was smart but she was beginning to feel like she didn't need school, a feeling Maurice, who hated school, knew well. She dropped out of high school, but she absorbed the culture of the house: She knew about Blake, Melville, Runge, Ensor, Mozart; she soaked in the casual conversation.

When she was sixteen her brother was moving out, and her mother and brother arranged that she would come and stay with Maurice, in the basement room under the studio. She never left, except for the seven years of her marriage, when she moved to another house on the property but still came and worked in the house all day long, cooking and eating dinner with Maurice. Even after she adopted her son, Nick, she brought him to live in the house and knock around while she worked. She was a servant and not a servant. She and Maurice would decide together what to have for dinner or what trees to plant. She was a part of the household in a way that could not be defined or pinned down with pedestrian words like "daughter" or "mother" or "friend" or "lover" or "assistant" or "housekeeper." When Maurice was asked in late interviews what exactly she was to him, he'd say, "She's my best friend. She is my most devoted friend. She sacrificed herself for me," or "She is the woman in my life," or "She puts up with my bad behavior."

In the last few years of Gene's life, when he got sick and stopped working in the city during the week, Lynn ran the house for both of them, catering to them, helping to navigate their moods and negotiate their clashes and misunderstandings, which was, to put it mildly, not an easy job. Was the constant caretaking of larger-than-life, kvetching theatrical characters worth it for Lynn? From certain outside vantage points, it looks as if she was sacrificing a lot, but for her it was not a sacrifice. She was not simmering or resentful. She liked what she got out of this dazzling household, and there is no doubt, with her and her son, Nick, and Gene and Maurice eating at the table on the porch, television blaring, dogs sprawled on the floor, that this was a family.

Lynn talks about what she did as "smoothing things out." She also talks about it as doing what had to be done so Maurice could work. He once said that working was "the only true happiness I've ever enjoyed. It's sublime ... where all of your weaknesses of character, and all blemishes of personality, and whatever else torments you fades away." If Maurice found his work to be the gravitational center of his life, so did Lynn.

In fact, her smoothing and straightening and caretaking reached the level of art itself. She says that if Maurice didn't have her, he could have hired someone else to do what she did, but it seems very unlikely that he would have found someone to match the power of her caretaking, the singular grace and intelligence of it.

Part of what made Lynn a superb companion for him was that she didn't try to save him or make him happy or take his unhappiness personally. She respected his moods; she helped him live with them; she enabled his patterns without wanting to change him, or believing change was possible, or secretly hoping for it. This sort of profound acceptance would have been impossible for a lover, or for most people, generally, but she realized that he worked within these swings and that the work was what mattered to him.

Sometimes, late at night, when she was in her room under Maurice's studio, Lynn could hear him whistling a whole opera—he was that talented at whistling—and stomping his feet, and she would drift off to sleep knowing that in the morning something great would be on his drawing desk. "That feeling of waking up and walking in and seeing something wonderful on the desk," she says. "That was magic."

Jonathan Weinberg, who usually talks a blue streak, is quiet in hospitals, and Danbury Hospital was no exception. He felt stricken and did not know what to say. "I probably looked like I was the one who was about to die," he says. Maurice joked about wanting to sleep with the handsome male nurse, maybe to cheer Jonathan up or to somehow say, "I'm still here!"

In a way it was as if Jonathan fell into Gene and Maurice's life in the manner of a character in a Sendak book, as if he flew or floated, arrived by dough airplane or sailboat on a beautiful night with a yellow moon; they did not obtain the boy in the usual way.

Gene had been Jonathan's mother's best friend. When his mother died, Jonathan went to live with Gene and Maurice and spent summers with them once he went to college. They were father figures to him. They taught him a kind of reverence and rigorousness toward art. When Jonathan was little, Maurice gave him his first watercolor set. He taught him to draw trees. He drew him a lion, which Jonathan kept but spilled things on.

For a while, Jonathan, who became a painter and an art historian, lived on the adjacent property that Maurice had bought, and even when he moved to New Haven, an hour away, he and his husband, Nick, went over with groceries and made dinner on Sunday nights.

If Gene and Maurice could have had a biological son, he probably would have been something like the eleven-year-old

Jonathan—funny, brilliant, anxious, artistic, charming, warm, sensitive, not terribly at home in the world—so it is interesting that fate threw him their way.

Maurice once said that if he had a son he would leave him at the A&P, and so the father-ish situation he found himself in with Jonathan was fraught. In interviews he always implied that he never wanted children, because he had to devote himself selfishly to his art, but he also needed too much undivided attention himself to have children around, clamoring for it.

They had a complicated closeness that fluctuated over the years, in the wild terrain of his affections, but Maurice wrote Jonathan once that he was like a son to him.

———

After the runaway success of *Where the Wild Things Are*, Maurice ran into a friend from Lafayette High School. She was the girl he sat next to in art class. On his high school yearbook page, which was captioned, "Your delightful drawings make us all gay. A famous artist you'll be someday," he had scrawled to her, "Lotsa luck to a swell gal. Sendak."

Now she said to him, "How does it feel to be famous?"

He said, "I still have to die."

———

Maurice had a passion for ritual. He liked to eat the same breakfast every day—marmalade, English muffin, tea—from nine to eleven, then he would work, then get dressed and walk the dog, then have lunch, then work, then dinner with cake, and then, from about ten to two in the morning, more work. The day was about creating a carapace for the work. In a letter to Minnie Kane, a reader with whom he warmly corresponded for decades, he once wrote that life was good when he was working or getting ready to work.

What is unsaid here is that life is not happy when he is not working. Like his mother and brother, Maurice had always wrangled with depression. The black moods would descend, and he would fight them off with work or, when he couldn't work, with the idea of work. The work was, among other things, a mood stabilizer. It kept him going; it lured and cajoled him back to life.

If Maurice was depressed, Lynn would tell him to get dressed and take the dog for a walk. He would say that he didn't want to get dressed, and she would coax him into doing it. One day Erda, one of the dogs, sensed his mood and wouldn't come near him, which put him into more of a funk.

Sendak often talked about his books as a "battleground" or "battles." In the hours in his studio, under the cheap white lamp clipped to his drawing desk, he was fighting. The business of creating children's books was not a sweet, civilized occupation; it was violent, bloody. He was defending or protecting himself.

"I'm totally crazy, I know that," he once said. "I don't say that to be a smartass, but I know that that's the very essence of what makes my work good." The craziness was in his work. The blackness was vital; he called it "the shadows." The shadows were in the illustrations. Without them, there would be only charm.

Those close to him sometimes heard the extremes of depression in his voice; he had more than a passing acquaintance with the edge. He smuggled moments of numbed depression into *Higglety Pigglety Pop!*—"The lion said, 'Please eat me up. There is nothing more to life'"—and into *My Brother's Book*—"For five long years he lay so sunk / Till bark enclosed his living trunk, / Bare vines entwined his glittering head. / Ask of the wild cherry tree: / Does he live? Is he dead?"

Maurice wrote a letter to Jonathan in the mid-seventies about being in a funk in San Francisco. He is working on a book that he thinks may be his best. This makes all the difference to his mood. He talks about the book as if it has entered the world to redeem him. He knows that the idea of art rescuing you is a cliché, but in this case, it's really true. He's going to make it because of the book.

This seems not an overstatement: The books and drawings and opera backdrops came to save him. Or he dreamed and labored to save himself.

219

While Maurice was in the hospital, Lynn talked to Jonathan about being more of a presence once Maurice got home. Jonathan agreed that he would come once a week, and maybe stay over, to help with his recovery.

Lynn told Maurice that they had redone the bathroom in the house to accommodate his loss of balance, but he was not interested in hearing about it. He was not talking about going home.

———

In the sixties, his intimations of mortality got very specific; his floating terror of death attached itself to specific losses. He began to work the deaths and illnesses of those close to him into his art.

Sendak was laid low by his white Sealyham terrier Jennie's illness in 1967. He would say later that Jennie was the love of his life, which was mostly a joke, but not entirely. The rawness blows through a bleak and howling letter he wrote to his friend Jan Wahl. He writes that he is staying home with Jennie because he is nervous about leaving her and is constantly checking that she is breathing. He says he drops to the ground and writhes. Destruction is everywhere, magnified. Caterpillars attacked a vine, and when he drenched them with insecticide, they trembled and thrashed on the ground as ants consumed them. He feels like death is everywhere and he is bad at life. He is so filled with self-contempt that he wonders how Jan can bear him.

Maurice's panic over Jennie's decline suffuses the book he was working on, *Higglety Pigglety Pop! Or, There Must Be More to Life*. Behind this was also his panic about his mother's cancer, though he said it was easier to be worried about the dog dying than his mother because the latter would be too huge and consuming. The darkness threatened to engulf him, and he tried to draw his way through it. He couldn't explain what was going on, he wrote in another letter to Jan Wahl about the book. He wrote about how grueling the writing process was, the toll it was taking on him. He is writing through a kind of blackness, both sure of his art and in great, unmanageable pain. He tells Jan not to worry about him, that this anguish is a reasonable price to pay for creative power. Even if the book doesn't succeed, it will have been worth it. The letter is an extraordinary mix of certainty and rawness, both harrowing and triumphant.

The book itself is shot through with pain; the terror of death is tamed like a dancing bear; it performs.

The illustrations are meticulous line drawings with elaborate cross-hatching, evoking another century. They are so intricately drawn they could almost be etchings. He traced over a photograph of Jennie to get her shaggy jowls exactly right. A creative, transformative kind of tracing over a light box was integral to his process.

The story flows with a dream logic: A dog leaves her owner, even though she had everything; she eats mind-boggling amounts of food, meets various animals, and ends up as the new nurse to Baby. Baby's parents have mysteriously left, and a lion downstairs has devoured the previous nurses, because they could not get Baby to eat. Jennie saves Baby, though not before she has her head in the lion's mouth, and she ends up as a star in the Mother Goose World Theatre at Castle Yonder. She writes a letter to her master, "Hello, As you probably noticed, I went away forever. . . . I can't tell you how to get to Castle Yonder because I don't know where it is. But if you ever come this way, look for me. Jennie."

Along the way, the odd, whimsical story gives voice to a very high level of bleakness, of nearly giving up. Take Jennie's conversation with the ash tree: Jenny wonders why the ash tree is complaining when it has everything. The ash tree cries, "The birds are gone, my leaves are dead, and I'll soon have nothing but the empty, frozen night."

But the story pulls back from the brink it is flirting with. There is a darkness lapping at the edges, a gloom being fought off, but it is so gloriously, stylishly fought off that one feels, in the end, consoled.

The softness of the drawings also plays against some of the more alarming bits of text. The cross-hatching almost reproduces the dog's shagginess; there is a furriness to the drawings, which comforts. There are no hard lines or angles; everything is shaded, gentle. There is a sweetness to the illustrations that answers some of the bleakness and wondering in the words.

The pain Maurice felt in this period morphs into a sharp, comic, wry production of the play *Higglety Pigglety Pop!* The stately elegance of the drawings collides with the silliness of the scene: "The pig is a top-hatted doctor who pours pills onto Jennie, who is lying on the floor. The cat comes in and says the lion is loose, and the pig jumps out the window, and the lion comes onstage to say, "Higglety" and "Pigglety," before Jennie pops him with a mop.

The idea of the afterlife as a rhyming absurdist play, where the dog eats salami mops as a famous star of the stage, is a great generous joke that only Sendak could dream up. There is in *Higglety Pigglety Pop!* a restorative, wholly sui generis charm. But the book does not do away with what Maurice elsewhere calls "the shadows."

In an early draft of the book, one can see the traces of his struggle to tackle loss. The early version ends on a more up-beat and less sublimely mystical note. Jennie's owner writes, in answer to her letter, that he had read an item about it in the newspaper, and promises to visit. The loss in the draft is not really a loss—it is too easily undone; the mystery, the beyond reach–ness, of Castle Yonder is dismantled in this version. But Maurice began to whittle the coda down in subsequent drafts and finally took it out entirely, scribbling in pencil that he should take it out because it is too solid and worldly. He wants the ending to tantalize and bewilder the reader.

In earlier drafts, the drawings on the final pages are also sweeter: All of the characters climb atop a lion and ride off together, as they do in Sendak's nutshell library story, *Pierre*. The ending is neater, prettier, cozier; the difficulty managed, glossed over, cute.

But as Sendak worked through the drawings, the ending became sharper, more eloquent. In the final version, we can only see the cat holding the lion's tail. The rest of the lion is out the window, offstage, unseen. The absurdity lingers, unchildproofed. The festive darkness, the exuberant bewildering frolic, is unhampered. There is no resolution in this version of the drawing, only buoyant mystery.

Tony Kushner writes of the book's ending: "'Pop! Stop! Clop! Chop! The End.' Samuel Beckett couldn't have put it more succinctly."

———

Tony came to see him at Danbury Hospital. He brought the opera *Le Cinesi* to play for him. Gluck had written it for the household of Empress Maria Theresa. Maurice loved listening to it. He told the nurses that he wanted to be addressed as Your Royal Highness Princess Amalia, who was one of Maria Theresa's daughters.

Maurice was infatuated with opera. He spent decades working on giant backdrops for huge productions of *The Magic Flute*, *Hansel and Gretel*, and *Brundibar*. He was drawn to the grand scale, the oversize, the exaggerated, the heroic; he reveled in the constant pitch of emotional intensity, the richness of feeling, the extravagant, lavish, too much–ness of it.

Tony was glad he liked the Gluck. Maurice seemed to him generally in pretty high spirits. He was doing physical therapy. It seemed to Tony that this was just an episode, like others he'd had in the past, but he would get better and go home and draw.

———

Here are some things Maurice had left behind in the studio when he left for the hospital: One of Lewis Carroll's photographs of the original Alice, when she was older and sulkier at the whole process of being photographed. Several of his Mickey Mouses from the thirties. An authentic Jewish star with the word JUDE on it. A beautiful forties'-style photograph of Ursula Nordstrom, his first editor (who looked at the first draft of *Where the Wild Horses Are*, with his failed attempt to draw horses, and observed acidly, "Maurice, what *can* you draw?" "Things," he said. "Things!"). A red cardigan draped around the back of his chair. A sepia photograph of himself as a child, taken by a photographer in the street, which irritated his mother because she had to pay for it.

———

Lynn offered to bring Sendak's dog Herman to Danbury Hospital to see him. She thought she could arrange it. The hospital was very aware of who Maurice was. But he refused. He didn't want to see the dog. That's when she knew he wasn't coming home.

———

Maurice had always been attuned to the idea that he might die suddenly, but his heart attack at age thirty-nine gave those misty fears tangible form. Afterward, he felt very uneasy being alone; he was worried that something would happen to him and he wouldn't be able to get to the hospital. For decades he was in reasonably good health, his heart ticking along without incident, but he had a strong feeling of impending calamity, of a fall, a collapse, a heart failure, a trip to the emergency room. He wrote in a letter to Minnie Kane on his fiftieth birthday that he is proud of being fifty, that he didn't think, after his heart attack at thirty-nine, that he would make it to such an advanced age.

He wrote about how defining this experience was in his journal: He says he hates May because it is the month of his heart attack. He says that he was born with his heart attack. He describes death as if it is a friend who is waiting for him.

Maurice's first heart attack caught him *in medias res*. He was on a publicity tour for *Where the Wild Things Are*, in England, in the countryside. It was May 1967. He was in the middle of filming a television show for the BBC, and he felt a radiating pain in his chest. He couldn't speak and had to leave the studio, though, this being England, they gave him a whiskey first. He went back to his hotel room to rest, and he wrote in his journal that he thought he was dying.

In the middle of the night he banged on his editor Judy Taylor's door and was taken to Queen Elizabeth Hospital in Gateshead-upon-Tyne, where he remained for weeks. The hospital staff doted on him and spoiled him. Judy gave him a stuffed mouse, which he named Judy.

In the midst of the ordeal, Gene flew over to be with him. When Maurice was a bit better, they moved him to recuperate for a few weeks in a nursing home in London. There he read all of Laura Ingalls Wilder's *Little House on the Prairie* books, which he found reassuring: "Calmly and clearly she illustrates the courage necessary to live an ordinary life. She is not concerned with fantasy heroics but with falling down and getting up, being ill and recovering. What is important, she says, is to continue. In persevering, you will discover triumphs. This is what I was searching for, what I found in her books. I wanted to learn how to behave admirably in adversity." He wrote a card to his friend Barbara Dicks, saying that he had been ready to blow his brains out in the hospital. Gene scribbled next to it, "or mine."

As he recovered his health in the shaky months that followed, he wrote an extraordinary letter to Minnie Kane, who had herself just suffered a loss. He said that now he could truly inhabit her sorrow, he himself having gone through it. He asks her to let him be with her in her mourning. He feels along with her. He says that together they will go through a "terrible strengthening." They will survive everything.

———

As it happened, the years following his heart attack did see him through a "terrible strengthening." They were harrowing but creatively fruitful; he faced down rafts of grief and fear and worked them onto the page. His mother died; his father was succumbing to the cancer that would kill him; Jennie died; and he poured all of it into the exuberant romp of *In the Night Kitchen*. He wrote to Minnie Kane that this would be one of his best books.

Drawing on the gleaming manic energy of the turn-of-the-century cartoonist Winsor McCay and the Mickey Mouse movies of his childhood, Sendak dreamed up a nighttime tableau of a boy named Mickey, who falls out of his bed, out of his clothes, through his house, past his mama and papa sleeping (or maybe having sex), and into a surreal kitchen where three fat bakers try to bake him into a cake.

The city itself is the giant kitchen, with skyscraper-sized orange juice cartons and jam jars and cake mixes and corkscrew towers against a gorgeous midnight-blue sky. The city—somehow more Brooklyn than Manhattan, with its elevated trains and low buildings, not grand or gleaming or modern but homey, seedy, down at the heels—is steeped in nostalgia, with a comforting, old-fashioned feel to everything, the writing on the labels, the glass milk bottle, belonging to the past.

The world glimmers, lost, forlorn, mysterious, under a fat yellow moon. His obsessions seep into the dreamscape: Jennie, his mother's death, his father's final decline, his heart attack.

The wild, beautiful night kitchen is landmarked with a flour sack that reads 1953. JENNIE. 1967 BAY SHORE L.I., which is where Gene eventually took Jennie to put her down after her cancer progressed while they were on Fire Island. There is a shortening sack that reads KILLINGWORTH, CONNECTICUT, which was Jennie's birthplace; an elevated train passes JENNIE STREET, and the face of the clock Mickey falls past in his house reads in tiny script: *Jennie.*

As Maurice worked endlessly on the illustrations—he made four dummy books, which were mock-ups of the originals, and countless drawings on tracing paper over light boxes, which was part of his exacting technique—his father, who was dying, moved into his apartment on 9th Street. His father was sleeping on a bed in his studio.

At his desk, he drew a giant can of tomatoes with a label reading PHILIP'S BEST. In another picture on the same page, a can, mostly obscured, bears the label SADIE'S BEST. And the book itself is dedicated to his parents, FOR SADIE AND PHILIP, with Mickey hovering in his dough plane next to the dedication.

He also drew into the book several private references to his own brush with death. There is a shortening sack with a label saying Q. E. GATESHEAD, which was the hospital he went to in England. There is a baking soda labeled PHOENIX BAKING SODA, which captures the rising-from-the-ashes spirit of those months of recovery.

In a television interview, when Sendak was nearing eighty, Bill Moyers says to him: "Are you obsessed with death?"

> Maurice Sendak: A little bit. It's such a curious thing.
> Bill Moyers: How so?
> MS: It's a whole adventure.

In *In the Night Kitchen*, there is a purplish flag fluttering atop a bottle in the distance, against the starry sky, that reads CHAMPION. This is a playful reference to one of the nurses at Gateshead calling him a "champion" as he was struggling for consciousness during his recovery. He felt like he was pulling a rope to get out of a well, and he heard her English accent, calling him a "champion." The harrowing memory appears in this banner, woven in, mysterious. Even if you don't know the references, the mood of quiet triumph pervades.

> BM: Did you think about the holocaust?
> MS: Of course, my parents would say to me when I was
>     late for dinner playing stoopball, "Your cousin Leo
>     doesn't play ball. He is in a concentration camp. He is
>     dead." I was shamelessly enjoying myself while they
>     were cooked in an oven.

In *In the Night Kitchen*, Sendak takes the image of children being cooked in an oven and makes it his own. The fat bakers, on the thrilling edge between scary and funny, are baking

Mickey into a pie and putting him in an oven, until he pops out and saves himself. He kneads the dough into an airplane and flies up a giant milk bottle. He dives naked into the bottle and emerges with the milk, crowing against the violet dawn, "Cock-a-doodle-doo!" The image of the child in the oven is made over into a fun one.

The grandeur of *In the Night Kitchen* pops up in answer to the child's vulnerability. There is an exaggerated, cartoonish, amped-up vision of transcendence. The book's pure joy is enhanced by its shadows of calamity, its implicit acquaintance with darkness, its undercurrent of melancholy; even the colors, the rich velvety blue night, deepen the comedy. Mickey vanquishes obstacles and enemies, evades and outflies death by cake. Survival is fun, with a tremor of sublimity, of subterranean awe, that gives the book its majesty.

In earlier drafts of the book, the brutality was a bit more pronounced. The words were written out by hand on a yellow legal pad, and there was a point where the bakers sing a little song about a head injury that kills him, but in subsequent drafts the song is removed, the darkness managed and controlled.

If you look closely at Mickey's expression—in his tiny kneaded-dough airplane, atop the giant milk bottle, high above the whole miraculous vista, with the tin measuring cup on his head—you see that it is unhappy or overwhelmed or daunted. Mid triumph, he is considering the terrible or uncomfortable or dispiriting things in the world.

BM: Isn't this a time for a certain kind of ripeness in your life? . . . After all you will never die, Maurice Sendak. I'm serious about that. . . . Most of us will live only as long as our grandchildren remember us. But you will never die.

MS: I got news for you. I am going to croak.

———

Maurice flamboyantly hated many things, and among those things were hospitals. He could barely even bring himself to visit people he was very close to, he hated hospitals so much, so Lynn was surprised that he was not complaining more about the hospital, in particular about the hospital food. He was on a diet of thickened liquids, but he would ask for more cranberry mash or whatever they served.

At home, what he loved to eat was cake. He ate enormous amounts of cake, especially, when he was younger, chocolate cake. When he was still working in the city, Gene would bring boxes from the excellent bakeries in the West Village when he came for the weekend. Maurice particularly liked the seven-layer cake from Jon Vie. Lynn would make him marble cakes, pound cakes, lemon cake; she had his mother's recipes for sponge cake, banana cake, and spice cake, and she would make those too. The comforts of childhood were still the salient ones.

From the hospital bed, Maurice took Lynn's hand. "I love you." She said, "I love you too."

232

"Please don't go. We'll eat you up, we love you so!" say the wild things to Max in one of Sendak's most immortal lines. Love here is terrifying, consuming, exhilarating; it is infinitely recognizable, even to small children, annihilating, seductive. It's the purest expression we have of the delirious violence of strong feeling. The British psychoanalyst Donald Winnicott once wrote that the mother must resist making love to or eating her child, which resonates because certain loves are so fierce and urgent, it feels as if you want to bite or eat or consume the object of that love.

Maurice said he dreamed up the idea of the wild things as an adult, at a shiva after someone had died, with his brother and sister. They were sitting around, laughing about their relatives from Europe. The relatives didn't speak English. Their teeth were yellow. They grabbed the children's cheeks. It was like they would gobble up Maurice and his siblings, along with everything else in the house. The wild things were Jewish relatives.

In fact, Sendak's books are filled with beasts that might eat you, often lions. There is the lion in *Higglety Pigglety Pop!*, a stately yet cryptic menace, who closes his jaws around Jennie's head; there is the lion in the nutshell library, who swallows Pierre and then, after being hit on the head with a folding chair and shaken up and down by a doctor, spits him out again on the floor; there is the bear in *My Brother's Book*, who bites the brother and kills him. The idea of being consumed by an animal is a code for death—that is, depending on the moment in Sendak's life, either easily reversible or not. He is playing here with a very basic primal fear—being swallowed by a beast, a child's fear—but it is also a fear of being consumed, obliterated; it is about the loss of self on the most grave and terrifying adult level. Can you be close to another person without being consumed?

He liked to say that when his sister gave him his first book, he bit it. This fits with his sensual apprehension of the universe, his physical devouring of people, places; he took things in more sensually than most—he hugged his friends, grabbed their noses, kissed them on the lips.

There is a moment in *Where the Wild Things Are* when Max gets lonely with the wild things, in his tent, in the great orange dusk, and wants to go where someone loves him best of all. For Max, that someone is his mother, who has made him a warm supper with a big slice of layer cake. She is one of the great reassuring presences of a mother in literature, but for Maurice, that person was never his mother. Did people love him best of all? He voraciously hungered to know that they did.

———

Lynn made apple crisp and brought it to Maurice in the hospital, because it was soft enough for him to eat.

———

Maurice was one of those confusing people who needed both unusual amounts of solitude and unusual amounts of attention. He needed to be left alone to work—or not alone but unbothered, unhampered, un-tied-down, preferably with someone stretched out reading in the room, or watching television, or puttering around. But he also needed unusual amounts of focused attention. He connected instantly and deeply; he seduced with his stories, with his outrageousness, with his greater-than-usual capacity to truly empathize. People, especially younger people, melted around him, around the creator of *Where the Wild Things Are*, which conjured ancient nights in pajamas, curled up with their mothers. He did not like his friends having husbands or wives or boyfriends around to divide their attention; he liked untrammeled affection, being the center of things; he liked to perform, to mainline love.

One of the notable effects Maurice had on other people was that they wanted to do things for him. He cultivated a certain helplessness: He was a terrible driver, so people would drive him places, or he couldn't be alone, so people would stay with him. But on top of this, people would just do things for him— scour the earth for some rare book or painting or object he wanted, for instance. Something deeper than his fame made people want to look out for him, some essence that drew people to him and fostered a very particular kind of devotion. Women especially wanted to take care of him. They threw themselves at him, thought of marrying him, brought him pies.

One day a crazy woman from Australia came and sat naked on the front lawn. He called the police, who said there wasn't much they could do, as she wasn't really hurting anyone. Finally Maurice said he would go out and talk to her. Lynn and

Gene thought he was nuts, but he went and took a walk with her. She told him she wanted him to put a French horn in his next book, so he did. He drew Ida playing a French horn in *Outside Over There*.

———

At the hospital, Maurice liked to have Henry James read aloud. The reader would often trip over one of the winding sentences, and they would laugh. Why did it have to be Henry James? Maurice had said, a couple of months earlier, in an interview, "I want to read as much Henry James as I can cram. Pain in the ass that he is."

———

In the documentary about Sendak's life, *Tell Them Anything You Want*, made by Spike Jonze and Lance Bangs, the film crew drives up the snowy road to his Connecticut house. They get out of the car. "Do you have any advice for young people?" they ask, camera rolling. "Quit this life as soon as you can!" shrieks Sendak, shaking or pretending to shake. "Get out! Get out!" He is joking, but there is something terrifying or ragged in his voice. The moment on film is electric because it feels out of control, as if a real wild thing has been momentarily unloosed against the slate Connecticut sky, the bare trees.

Most adults would be incapable of an outburst like that, because they are too constrained; they cannot let such a primal expression into the open; they are not unleashing on the level that Sendak was able to unleash. Or maybe he was closer to that pain, had more direct access to a deeper self than most people do.

Sendak had always been a natural performer, a great story-teller, a charismatic talker, and a prolific charmer. There were always shocking bursts, a story that his listener could not believe he would be telling, but they were carefully moderated, superbly hilarious. Part of his magnetism was his outrageousness, his readiness with salaciousness, with irreverence, with a brilliantly deployed willingness to say something you are not supposed to say. When he received a National Medal of Arts at the White House, Bill Clinton told him that as a child he always imagined that he would grow up and wear a long coat with brass buttons. Sendak said, "Well, Mr. President, you only have one more year in office. You have plenty of time to pursue your dream of being a doorman."

One gets the sense that Sendak was crafting a persona for himself as carefully as any of the line drawings he did in his books. He was creating a character of Sendak, brilliant, dark, shocking, that would intrigue, provoke admiration, elicit deep love and loyalty, bind people to him in a way that they are rarely bound.

In his interviews and talks, Maurice presented uncheerful facts with varying degrees of comic acceptance. Most of the time they were assimilated into his mordant persona, darkly humorous, controlled, witty, adult. But occasionally, in his late interviews, there was a howl, a sorrow that was not managed, a wind that blew through what he was saying. In an interview he did with Terry Gross of National Public Radio in September 2011, he talks about two friends who had just died: "And when they die they are out of my life. They're gone forever. Blank. Blank. Blank." In the documentary, when a painful childhood memory comes up he says, "I cannot cry. I cannot talk about it." The rawness is startling, the flicker of jagged rage or pain. These moments are fascinating to watch, because they are unprocessed, untouched by the considerable managing intellect. For a second, there is just despair.

———

In March 2012, Tony Kushner's father died. He died at home, surrounded by loved ones, at peace. When Tony was talking to Maurice about it on the phone, Maurice began to weep; he was crying so much that Tony asked him why he was so upset: It made sense that he would be upset—his close friend's father had died—but why *that* upset? Maurice said it was because his death was so "decent." Was he thinking that he wasn't decent? That this kind of decency wasn't available to him?

———

In his last interviews over the winter, Sendak seemed overall to be crafting the image of an old man at peace with the universe. His closest friends heard his Terry Gross interview and thought, Who is that man? The dignified posture of Buddha-like acceptance seemed distinctly un-Maurice-like, though as Tony put it, he was "working toward it."

In that interview he said things like "I am not afraid of death," and "You know, there's something I'm finding out as I'm aging—that I am in love with the world. And I look right now, as we speak together, out my window in my studio and I see my trees, my beautiful, beautiful maples," and "Oh, God, there are so many beautiful things in the world which I will have to leave when I die, but I'm ready, I'm ready, I'm ready."

Still he had bursts of grouchiness, of wildness, of irreverence that winter. "Look at nature," he said in another interview. "How beautiful when she isn't having a fucking nervous breakdown and killing all of your trees."

Tony remembers going for a walk with him. Maurice was in the middle of telling him that he had stopped caring about his reputation, about what people thought of him, about whether he was a great artist; none of this mattered to him anymore. It was all vanity and he was at peace, and he had started to love trees and care about the things he'd overlooked before. Just then a car pulled up next to them. One of his neighbors rolled down the window and started to talk about how she had seen another "kiddie-book writer," Jim Henson, on television. Maurice cringed at the phrase "kiddie-book writer" and launched into an obscenity-laced rant against Henson, who he felt had stolen some ideas from him. So he hadn't quite given up the worldly chatter. Kushner once called his wrath "scorching as dragon's breath," and the heat was still there.

In a television interview in January, in Sendak's living room, Stephen Colbert tried to badger and shock, but Sendak, cane leaning against his chair, was his superbly wicked self. "Do you like them?" Colbert asks, referring to children. "I like them as few and far between as I do adults, though maybe a bit more because I really *don't* like adults." Colbert flips through the pages of *Where the Wild Things Are*. "Is rumpus sex?" "Yes . . . your mother screaming. Your father saying 'shut up.'" When Colbert questions the nakedness of the boy in *In the Night Kitchen*, Sendak says, "Have you never had a dream yourself where you were totally naked?" Colbert says no, and Sendak says drily, "You're a man of little imagination." Later in the interview, Sendak starts singing "Remember Pearl Harbor." You can see the respect in Colbert's eyes. The eighty-three-year-old children's book writer has been funnier than him.

Which is closer to the real mood of those last months, the wily black humor of the Colbert interview or the dignified gray eminence of the Terry Gross interview? It's absurd to think any interview plumbs the depths, but both contain bits of his evolving attitude, glimmers of him at eighty-three, still madly eloquent, still game.

———

In 2006 Maurice dug out an old idea for *Bumble-Ardy* and worked on it while Gene was dying of lung cancer in the house. They had set up a bed in the dining room. Gene had four nurses and Lynn to take care of him. Maurice wanted to pitch in, but Gene mostly wanted Lynn to do the caretaking, and Maurice would increasingly escape to his drawing desk. "I did

*Bumble-Ardy* to save myself," he said. "I did not want to die with him."

As Sendak was doing the drawings, the artist he was playing with in his mind was James Ensor, a nineteenth-century Belgian painter whose moody canvases are full of skeletons at festivities, of mad, colorful, chaotic, terrifying masked balls. They feel like what would happen if Van Gogh had a nightmare about attending a party. Maurice liked the mood.

Maurice viewed artistic influence as an active process. He picked an artist to borrow from for many of his projects. As he put it, "The muse does not come pay visits, so you go out stalking, hoping that something will catch you. Where do I steal from?" As Jonathan put it, "He had a way of swallowing an artist whole, but what he came out with was wholly his own, unmistakably a Sendak drawing." The artist he swallowed for *Bumble-Ardy* was Ensor.

*Bumble-Ardy* is the story of a pig whose parents die when he is little. He is never allowed to have birthday parties, and he goes to live with his aunt Adeline, who loves him. While she is at work, he organizes an elaborate costume party for pigs. "*Bumble-Ardy* was a combination of the deepest pain and the wondrous feeling of coming into my own, and it took a long time," he told Terry Gross during the NPR interview.

The forbidden party Bumble-Ardy pulls together is magnificent. The masked pigs are tumbling into all sorts of wildness;

there is a disturbing disjunction between the smiling masks and the staring, serious eyes.

There is a gorgeous, haunted quality to the festivities, a frenzied jubilation, an eerie garishness, tambourines, pigs covered in stars, backgrounds very dark, almost purple. The mood is celebration in duress, mayhem under a shadow. There is a great pressure in the drawings. There is, in most of the pictures, one pig in a skeleton costume, playing a horn, or reaching out for a cupcake.

Finally Adeline comes home and is furious, and she chases the pigs out with a knife, threatening to turn them into ham. She says, "Okay smarty you've had your party! But never again!" A tearful Bumble says, "I promise! I swear! I won't ever turn ten!" There is a rapprochement on the next page, but this cryptic note feels like the real ending: Will Bumble refuse to age, to move forward? Will Bumble just give up? Will Bumble die?

Later, Maurice would say of *Bumble-Ardy* to Dave Eggers, "This is obviously the work of a man who has dementia. But I'm very happy with it."

Even after they had arranged for hospice care in the house, Maurice did not quite accept that Eugene was about to die. He would ask Lynn about treatments, even though Gene was very clearly beyond treatments. The flock of nurses hovered. Jonathan photographed and drew Gene. Jonathan read *Through the Looking-Glass* aloud to him.

242

One day Jonathan went for a walk with Maurice. It began pouring while he was telling Maurice that it was too late for treatments, that Gene was dying now. Maurice dissolved into tears. He collapsed. Jonathan had to help him into the house, his T-shirt soaked with rain.

When he was about to die, Gene suddenly wanted to go to the hospital, even though they had made hospice arrangements in the house. But he was worried about Maurice. He knew Maurice would not want him to go. Lynn told him not to worry about that, that she would talk to Maurice and that it would be all right. Gene was thinking even in that moment of how this decision would affect Maurice, but he couldn't stay in the house and die at home with Maurice, as Maurice had wanted. This seemed to Lynn like a snapshot of their relationship: how entwined but apart they were.

After Eugene died, Maurice wanted Lynn to take photographs of his body. He held on to these photographs and liked having them.

Eugene was cremated and his ashes were buried in the garden with Jennie, under a piece of a gravestone from a Jewish cemetery in Poland someone had brought. Maurice wanted to be buried there too. He had a terror of being buried with his mother and spending eternity with her.

Eugene's death walloped Maurice. There was a period of deep grief that followed. He couldn't sleep. He had nightmares. He felt guilty. He was unmoored. There is a pig in *Bumble-Ardy* with a stubbly hobo mask, holding a stick with a handwritten sign: WHERE DO WE GO FROM HERE?

In order to amuse Maurice in the year following Gene's death, Jonathan, who was living on the adjacent property with Nick, began to organize drawing "classes," though they weren't really classes. He and a couple of artist friends would find a male model on Craigslist and hire him to come up from the city. That afternoon Maurice would call, "Well, is he coming?" or "What does he look like?" and then he'd wander in an hour late, Herman in tow, and begin a large charcoal drawing of the nude model. Jonathan would tell Maurice not to mention who he was, so that it wouldn't somehow get out in the world as a gossip item—"Renowned Children's Book Illustrator Hires Nude Model from Craigslist"—but Maurice would begin talking to the model and somehow the name of one of his books would slip out. One of the models even ended up sending Maurice his own illustrations for a children's book. Maurice got a kick out of the whole thing. Sometimes he would stop drawing and just talk. He loved the casualness of four men standing around, charcoaling a nude, the safely erotic charge of it. He told Jonathan that when he could no longer see a handsome man walk by and feel desire, he would be ready to die.

———

Maurice liked to watch medical shows. He would be happy sitting at the dinner table, watching a graphic reality-TV surgery show while eating spaghetti. Someone sitting with him might wonder why he liked watching a human body ripped open, what he wanted to see.

On some level this could be seen as research, as Sendak belaboring a problem that obsessed him. He had always worked extraordinarily hard. He did more drafts, more dummy books, more tracings over light boxes, more fully realized drawings for his opera backdrops than he needed to, than other artists would, than necessity demanded; he labored toward the final version; he fought for it. His mastery of so many different styles and his vast strides in technical achievement are not a mystery: He worked insanely hard for them, and he was also working, in his own vivid way, on death.

Tony wrote about a conversation he had with Maurice:

> I tell him I will visit him in Connecticut. "Great," he says. "We can dance a kazatzkah!"
> "What kind of dance is that?" I ask.
> "A kazatzkah is the Dance of Death," he tells me.
> "Sounds good. Do you know the steps?" I ask.
> "Do I know them," he says with glee, making a kazatzkah sound like the most fun imaginable, "I know those steps in every notch, every noodle, every nerve cell! Of course I know them! I've been rehearsing them all my life!"

Sendak had collected a series of beloved objects that dealt with death: Mozart's letter to his father telling him that his mother was dead. A Chagall funeral scene. A grief-struck letter he wrote at sixteen to his future self on the day Franklin Delano Roosevelt died, full of lavish adolescent sorrow, railing against the people who just chattered and laughed as if nothing had happened. Wilhelm Grimm's letter "Dear Mili," to a child whose mother had died.

These objects were soaked in meaning for him. It was as if he had traveled somewhere and brought home souvenirs.

Maybe the most startling of these objects is Keats's original death mask. Maurice did not keep the wooden box containing it in his bedroom but in the blue guest room. He liked to open it and stroke the smooth white forehead. He said it did not make him feel sad, it made him feel maternal.

Maurice drew Eugene after he died, as he had drawn his family members when they were dying. The moment is one he was compelled to capture, pin down, understand, see. Where many—maybe most—people look away, he wanted to render. He was very wrapped up in the goodbye, the flight, the loss; it was almost Victorian, to be so deeply entranced with the moment of death, the instinct to preserve or document it. It's also the artist's impulse: to turn something terrible into art, to take something you are terrified of and heartbroken by and make it into something else. For the time it takes to draw what is in front of you, you are not helpless or a bystander or bereft: You are doing your job.

He talked to Jonathan about a famous Goya painting they both loved, of the artist with his doctor. Goya looks like he is about to shuffle off the mortal coil, clutching the bedsheet, and the doctor is behind him, cradling his shoulder and offering him a drink. In fact, Goya is cured, but the scene very much resembles a deathbed scene, a dying man lovingly held by his friend. Talking about the painting, in a lively conversation about art that he had with Jonathan at the New School, Maurice said: "It's so visceral. It makes me feel exalted."

But why "exalted"? He seems to have found something freeing or exhilarating about looking at something that so deeply frightened and compelled him; he wanted to gaze into it.

Apropos of this, he wrote another beautiful letter to Minnie Kane in 1964. He tells the story of visiting an old family friend who was dying. He was very afraid of seeing her, afraid of how his parents would feel, and afraid of how he would feel. This was the last time he would see her. And yet when he did it was strangely lovely. It was like staring into something he had always been terrified of, and it was exquisite. He left feeling both miserable and elated.

This seems to be key: Staring into something you have always been terrified of and finding it beautiful.

———

## MAY 3

Tony brought proofs of *My Brother's Book* to the hospital, for Sendak to look at and comment on for his publisher.

*My Brother's Book* is not a book anyone could believe was for children. It is strange and vibrant. Trees and sky dissolve into ribbons of color. It is as if Sendak is in a private conversation with Blake.

Maurice was passionately entwined with his brother when they were growing up. He often said his brother, Jack, was the better artist, and the two wrote a book together as kids; as teenagers they made intricate wooden toys of characters like Aladdin and Red Riding Hood, which they tried to sell to FAO Schwarz. The toy-store people were impressed with the ingenious designs but didn't think they could be mass-produced. His brother, who like their mother struggled with depression, never became an artist and worked in the post office. He died in 1995. "He was probably a genius," Maurice said. "But he was severely handicapped."

The brother in *My Brother's Book* dies. The brother tells a bear that he can eat him if the bear can answer a riddle. The bear asks him what kind of riddle. The boy says, "A sad riddle is best for me."

February was the month Maurice's brother died and the month Gene was born. The boy says, "In February it will be my snowghost's anniversary." This echoes an earlier, happier line from *Chicken Soup with Rice:* "In February it will be my snowman's anniversary, with cake for him and soup for me. Happy once. Happy twice. Happy chicken soup with rice."

248

When the bear eats him, the boy flies naked through the air. The flying through the air is a graceful rendition of something possibly more painful or brutal.

There are lots of stars in Sendak's late books. As the brother dies, the stars burst over the page.

—

Lynn's impression was that Maurice was not brave about the little things, but he was brave about the big things. He wrestled with terrible back pain for decades, but he did not complain about that, even though he was what Tony calls a "champion lamenter." He was once supposed to go into the city for an interview with a woman who had come all the way from Sweden, but he had her come up to see him instead, because he had an ingrown toenail, which was bothering him. When the woman's van arrived and her husband wheeled her down a ramp, Maurice realized that he had forgotten she was paralyzed. He had made a paralyzed woman who came all the way from Sweden to talk to him drive up to Connecticut! He felt terrible and apologized profusely, and she said, "Well, I imagine an ingrown toenail would be painful if I could feel my toes."

—

In early April, before the hospital, Tony had been talking to Maurice on the phone while he was recovering from cataract surgery. He couldn't see properly and he had a terrible head-ache and his back pain was worse than usual, and he sounded bleaker than Tony had ever heard him. He said he couldn't draw if he couldn't see. He said that there was no reason for him to be alive. Tony was starting to get worried, and he asked where Lynn was; Maurice said he didn't know and he was alone in the house. Tony told him to wait and he would drive up to Connecticut, so he got in the car and drove. He called Lynn but she didn't answer her phone. When he pulled up to the house, the car was gone. The door was open, and when Tony walked in, Herman started to bark. Otherwise, the house was quiet. Tony made his way through the empty rooms, be-coming more and more alarmed, and then he came to Mau-rice's studio. There was Maurice, covering one eye with his hand, stooped over his drawing desk, working away on the drawings for *The Nose Book*. He was slightly abashed that Tony had driven all the way up, but only slightly.

*The Nose Book* is the book Sendak was working on in these last months. He hadn't gotten very far into it. But the book merrily takes on the subject of bodily assault, of the sort of alienation from one's body that older people are increasingly familiar with. A boy's nose is stolen.

Maurice loved noses, and he loved Tony's nose in particular. In fact, Maurice loved Tony's nose so much that Tony had a bust made of it on the set of one of his movies, and he gave it to Maurice as a gift. It was a classic Jewish nose, which had been broken and bent to one side. Maurice loved to bend it the other way, pretending to fix it.

250

He had always wanted to write a poem about a nose, but when he was younger, he thought it would be too silly. At this point in his life, he didn't care.

The penciled writing is spidery. The illustrations are water-color over pencil; the lines are less precise, less controlled, than in his earlier work, but the drawings, with their splashes of color, are unmistakably Sendakian: gleeful, wicked, irre-pressible. There is the water taxi carrying Capri Island cops speeding off, and noses dangling from the sky, with signs an-nouncing FREE NOSES, evoking Sendak mischief at its best. The arc of the story is that a mother who does something wrong to her child is forgiven. This is the unfinished business on his drawing desk.

———

One morning at the hospital, Maurice told Lynn that he had a dream about her: She is lying on a sofa draped in white sheets, and behind her is a wall painted with an elaborate Dickensian Christmas scene. There is a vista of a small town covered in snow, a horse-drawn carriage. It is a wonderful peaceful scene.

Lynn pointed out that Maurice hated Christmas—he once said in an interview, "I hate this fucking holiday so much I can't tell you"—and he hated snow, but he said it was a beautiful, com-forting dream.

Maurice really did hate and fear snow. Everyone else would talk about how pretty it was, with the house nestled in powdery drifts, but he would call snow "white death." He was worried he would have a heart attack and not be able to get to the hospital and would die. When it snowed, he and Lynn would bundle up and go outside and get the snow off the roof, which he was afraid would collapse from it, and brush it off the bushes, which he thought would die from the weight.

So this comforting dream about a snowy scene was a dream about "white death." The feeling of Christmas, which had always alienated and irritated him with its foreignness, its exotic exclusion, had turned sweet.

It is interesting that comfort would come to Maurice via a painted wall. He didn't dream the Christmas scene itself but a painting of the scene; his imagination would render this comfort in a backdrop, like the opera backdrops he labored so intensively over for years. His subconscious was still painting.

———

## MAY 4

At around five, Lynn came back to Maurice's room from getting coffee, and he looked strange. There was something strange about the way he was holding himself. He couldn't move one whole side of his body. Lynn knew immediately that something was wrong and called the doctor. It turned out that he'd had another stroke.

When he was going in for the MRI, Maurice looked scared. Lynn felt awful. She asked their doctor, who was by now his friend and a familiar face, if he could go in with him, but that was against protocol. She hated for him to be alone.

———

Maurice had seen peaceful deaths. "When my father was dying, he'd dwindled—he had the body shape of a boy—and as I held him, I noticed that his head had become bigger than the rest of him and was rolling back like an infant's. Death at that moment was like going to sleep. 'Shhhh, it will be all right.' It's what you'd say to a feverish baby, except that he was dead."

After that, the scene took a manic Sendakian turn when Maurice wanted to see his father's penis. Without thinking, he began to undress him. His brother, alarmed, said, "What are you doing?" and Maurice said, "Papa's penis is where we come from. Don't you want to see it?" "No!" his brother shouted. Here you can almost see Mickey, sliding naked down the giant milk bottle in *In the Night Kitchen*, crowing, "Cock-a-doodle-doo!"—millions of children shocked, titillated, riveted.

———

As a child, Maurice was obsessed with the Lindbergh-baby kidnapping. He was three and a half when the baby was kidnapped, and he heard the news blaring from the radio. He thought, if this rich, Gentile, cherished blond baby could be taken from his house, what hope could there be for a poor sickly Jewish kid like him? He remembered the teary voice of the baby's mother on the radio, pleading with the kidnappers to rub camphor on the baby's chest because he had a cold. The news story merged with some apprehension already forming in his head: Babies could be lost, could vanish, could be stolen, could die.

He would later draw the Lindbergh baby, who did in fact die, in one of his more alarming books, *Outside Over There*, where a baby is stolen by faceless goblins; they creep through a window, like the Lindbergh kidnappers, and replace the baby with one made of ice. In a scene mimicking Maurice's own childhood, the baby is left in the care of her older sister, Ida, while the mother gazes indifferently off into the distance. She is very clearly, but for mysterious reasons, not responsible for the infant. Though the baby is stolen by goblins and then returned, the mother remains deeply, eerily disinterested.

In adult life, Maurice became very interested in obtaining one of the kidnapper's macabre little ladders, which were sold as souvenirs during his New Jersey trial. He went to great lengths to obtain it. When he finally got it, though, in 2009, he wasn't sure what to do with it. He wasn't really comfortable owning it, and kept it in the shed.

His own theory about the Lindbergh case was that the baby was killed by his father and the entire kidnapping story was a cover-up. He privately told friends that it was shaken-baby syndrome. What obsessed him, then, was not a story about a child stolen out of the window of his family's home but a terrible hidden act of family violence.

254

He reveled in a letter a little girl wrote to him about *Outside Over There:* "'Why did you write this book? This is the first book I hate. . . . I hope you die soon. Cordially.' A letter like that is wonderful. 'I wish you would die.' I should have written back, 'Honey, I will; just hold your horses.'"

———

One day, when he was around six, Maurice was playing ball with his friend Lloyd in the alley behind his house, laundry strung from the windows above their heads. He threw the ball too high, and Lloyd missed and it bounced and rolled into the street. Lloyd ran after it, and Maurice watched as a car hit him and he went flying through the air.

Seven decades later, in a television studio, he could not talk about Lloyd easily. His voice thickened. "I remember Lloyd like flat out in the air." He held his arms out to the sides to demonstrate. "It could be a distorted memory, but I see the arms and the head; he's flying."

Right here is the act of imagination: He has turned dying into flying. The brutal or traumatic thing he had witnessed becomes another thing, less brutal and traumatic, ambiguous.

Maurice was sure it was his fault and ran upstairs and locked himself into his room; even later, when Lloyd's mother sat with him on the stoop and told him it wasn't his fault, he was still sure it was his fault. He kept in his head the picture of the car hitting Lloyd and the dead boy flying through the air.

In his illustrations, he would take the picture of a child flying through the air and make it beautiful; the flying became floating—it is supremely tranquil, graceful, slow. There is an element of mystery suffusing it, a supernatural aura to it, but it is not frightening. The idea of falling or floating out of life is saturated with quiet excitement.

What does it mean for children to vanish or fall out of mundane life? Think of Mickey falling out of his bed, out of his clothes, through the air, past his mama and papa's bedroom in *In the Night Kitchen;* it is a slow, pretty, festive falling he is doing. Think of Ida floating through the air to find the baby stolen by goblins in *Outside Over There,* elegant in the folds of her gold cape, still holding her French horn. Think of the brother in *My Brother's Book,* who also floats naked through the air, to his death, admittedly, but in a graceful way. Think of the naked boy floating upside down through his house in the collaboration with Randall Jarrell, *Fly by Night.* The searing image is recast as a happy exit from the ordinary world.

A boy flying out of life might be a good thing.

——

Maurice said once in an interview: "I want to be alone and work until the day my head hits the drawing table and I'm dead. Kaput." And he had discussed with Lynn and his doctor that when he couldn't work or walk his dogs, he would be ready to die.

Now the doctor was honest about his situation: After this second stroke, they could do more physical therapy, more rehab, but there was no chance he could walk on his own or write, and there was a high likelihood that he would have another stroke. He asked Maurice if he still felt the way they had discussed. Maurice nodded.

After that, he went into a large "comfort care" room, which was essentially hospice care.

———

That last winter he was reading a biography of Blake. "I read Blake because I want to schlep something from him that I can eat raw, *have*," he said. "My life is my work. Why am I clinging to every word Blake says in this book? I'm trying to suck all his strength out."

Sendak was particularly enthralled by the image of Blake seeing angels and sitting up and singing on his deathbed: "He's lying in bed, he's dying, and all the young men come—the famous engravers and painters—and he's lying and dying, and suddenly he jumps up and begins to sing! 'Angels, angels!'" He loved the idea of this, as if it was an imaginative tour de force, an almost artistic achievement, that he could see angels in front of him.

Once, in the seventies, Maurice was up in the middle of the night, wandering around the living room. Lynn heard him and came up and asked him if he was okay. He said that he had heard something thumping, and when he went downstairs it was a bat flying around the living room, and the bat had sat next to him on the couch and spoken to him for a long time in German. "Do you believe me?" She tried to laugh it off, but he kept asking. She knew he wanted her to say yes, and so she did. The bat was real to him, he was telling her. How far would she follow him, he was asking, how far would she go in seeing what he saw? He was used to pushing the edges of the imagination. He was used to seeing—in great, gorgeous, physical detail—things that were not there.

In a moment of mischief, he told an interviewer that he wanted "a yummy death," like Blake's. "He died a happy death," he explained. "It can be done. If you're William Blake and totally crazy."

In fact, Sendak had a history of seeing angels. When Maurice was very sick in bed as a child, his father told him that if he looked out the window he would see an angel, and that angel would be a sign he would get better. He stared out the pane, then caught the barest glimmer of one. He told his father he had seen it. That meant he would get better. The idea that you could see an angel, or be an angel, or create an angel, as his grandmother did when she dressed him in white, was part of his family mythology.

Maurice liked the idea of believing, even though he didn't believe. He didn't believe in an afterlife. He didn't believe in God. When an interviewer asked him, at eighty-three, what came next, he said, "Blank. Blank. Blank." But he had such an intense imaginative life that he sometimes couldn't help conjuring some sort of world or presence in that blankness. "I feel very much like I want to be with my brother and sister again. They're nowhere. I know they're nowhere and they don't exist, but if nowhere means that's where they are, that's where I want to be." And, "I don't believe in an afterlife, but I still fully expect to see my brother again. And it's like a dream life." He draws the bountiful orange waterfall, like trees of the mystical place past life, in *My Brother's Book*. He draws the stage of the Mother Goose World Theatre in *Higglety Pigglety Pop!* His imagination won't stop. When faced with "Blank. Blank. Blank," the artist in him draws.

―――

## MAY 6

Maurice had slipped into unconsciousness. He had said he didn't want visitors, except his very closest friends, and Lynn had kept them at bay, but now that he seemed unaware of his surroundings, friends began to flow in: Twyla Tharp, Spike Jonze, old friends, neighbors, young illustrators, along with Jonathan and Nick and Tony.

―――

## MAY 7

There were about twenty people in the room. After a while, Lynn felt that Maurice needed more peace in the room, so she asked them to leave. It was unlike her to ask people to leave—it was more like her to get everyone sandwiches—but she had a strong feeling that Maurice needed them to leave.

Lynn had listened to his breathing on a baby monitor for the past few years, as he was afraid something would happen to him in the night and no one would hear. She heard his breathing in her dreams, in the background of her thoughts as she lay in bed. She'd absorbed its rhythms as if it were almost part of her, so when it was his last breath she knew. She didn't wait for another breath. She called a nurse. "Did he just die?" The nurse said yes. The time was 2:45 A.M.

She was surprised by the expression of peace on his face. He looked more at ease than he had in life. Something had happened. Something had shifted. But who would draw him?

# Epilogue: James Salter

James Salter opens the refrigerator of his small Bridgehampton kitchen and pours me a glass of iced tea. He is wearing a denim shirt. His eyes are the color of a noon sky.

Once we settle down with our iced teas on wicker chairs on the screened porch, I am aware that there is something unseemly about asking a thriving, eighty-nine-year-old writer to talk about death. He is aware of my awareness.

"I am here," he says. "I agreed to talk to you."

One of the reasons I am attracted to Salter is his absolute clarity. In a *New Yorker* profile, a friend of his describes him with Graham Greene's line, "The writer must have a tiny sliver of ice in his heart," and he does seem to have a tiny sliver of ice in his heart in the best possible way.

Like all the conversations I had for this book, this is not a standard interview. It is not clear actually that it is an interview at all. I emailed him that I wanted to talk to him about death though I very much understood if he didn't feel like it, and he said yes.

In some larger sense, of course, the thing I want from him is delusional. I want him to tell me what it means to come up close to death. He flew fighter planes in Korea. He writes more radiant sentences than any writer alive. He seems from his fiction to see ends in beginnings, loss before the fact. From these unrelated details, I have somehow concocted a fantasy that he has made peace with death, seen it up close, knows its surface. I have a further implausible fantasy that he can or wants to share this knowledge with me and put it into words.

At many points on the bus ride to see him, I think, What am I doing? I had thought about what to bring and am carrying a box of cookies from a bakery near me in Brooklyn, which seems patently not the right thing to bring for a talk about death with a hard-as-nails old writer you admire, but I am nonetheless carrying the beribboned brown box.

Salter's last novel, *All That Is*, is lean, muscular, vital. He does not seem, in his sentences, to be in anything but his prime, though he was in fact in his late eighties when he wrote it. "I just wrote it," he says. "I thought I would try something and that was it."

Salter has not lost his smashing good looks, though age has softened them. He once wrote about a beautiful woman: "The years had seized and shaken her as a cat shakes a mouse."

*The New Yorker* called its profile of him "The Last Book." But maybe it isn't his last book?

"I don't know if I'll keep writing," he says. "I write things, but I don't know."

———

"To tell you the truth, I don't think much about death," he says.

This I wasn't expecting. How can you be eighty-nine and not think about death? Not to mention that his work is obsessed with transience and has been since he was young.

He says, "I thought about death more when I was thirty than before or after."

"Why thirty?" I ask. "What happened then?"

"I don't know."

Salter is looking at me as if he is in the pilot's seat and I am on the ground.

He is not naturally, chattily introspective, like a male novelist my own age would be. He is willing to talk about himself in a way, but it is not the familiar outpouring of "then I felt" and "then later I started feeling" and "then I started to be much more comfortable with . . ." that would stream from a younger male novelist; Salter's own carefully calibrated emotions do not seem to him like the hot center of the universe from which all things flow.

I try something else. "Your work seems very interested in preserving a moment, very alert to death."

"The work," he says. "Yes."

In *All That Is*, he writes: "There was a time, usually late in August, when summer struck the trees with dazzling power and they were rich with leaves but then became, suddenly one day, strangely still, as if in expectation and at that moment aware. They knew. . . . The sun was at its zenith and embraced the world, but it was ending, all that one loved was at risk."

Even the scenes he wrote when he was much younger, in his novels *A Sport and a Pastime* and *Light Years* and in his collection *Dusk and Other Stories*, are infused with a presentiment of loss, are sharpened and glorified by it. Everything he writes is elegy, a paean to a moment as it is in the process of being lost. Dusk is his language.

Even his famous sex scenes between a Yale dropout and a French girl in *A Sport and a Pastime* are somehow more intense because the man leaves her, as we know he will, and then dies in a car crash. Salter writes each evening, each dinner of soup, oysters, cheese, wine, each dirty scene, each hotel room strewn with clothes, as if it's the last night on earth, and that mood is what draws me.

"My first death was my grandfather's," Salter says. "I didn't know him well. I knew what I was supposed to feel, but I didn't feel very much. My father didn't appear to either. We never talked about it. I didn't know what to do but to appear to feel."

Later he went to West Point. He was there during World War II. Very young and training for the army, he took a masculine, romantic view of death. He had a picture of his roommate's older brother, who had become a fighter pilot, and his wife. He wrote, "When he was killed on a mission not long after, I felt a secret thrill and envy. His life, the scraps I knew of it, seemed worthy, complete. He had left something behind, a woman who could never forget him; I had her picture. Death seemed the purest act. Comfortably distant from it I had no fear."

He tells me the deaths he encountered in the army didn't shake him or touch him. "To be honest, I was invigorated by those," he says. "They authenticated me."

This reminds me of Sontag after her first cancer, of how her closeness to death made her giddy, how she wrote that it was "fantastic" to brush up next to it. "Fantastic." "Invigorated." "Authenticated." These are not words you'd expect to crop up in a conversation about death. But they are describing the energy that comes from coming up close to death and not dying. "It's like when you see a car crash and it reminds you for a moment," Salter says. "The realization that certain things are possible. It doesn't last."

"What was that line you have in *Burning the Days* about the soldiers you knew who died? They were like water under the oar?"

Salter says, "Oar swirl."

I notice that he remembers and can quote every single line I refer to. The line is about an older cadet named Benny Mills who dies in 1944: "His death was one of many and sped away quickly, like an oar swirl."

Oar swirl. The surface of the water ripples and then is calm.

———

"Do you ever imagine what a death is like?" I ask.

"No," he says. "I don't try to imagine it."

But while we are talking, I can't help but notice he imagines at least two specific deaths. He lapses, almost automatically, into imagining them. He writes them like a novelist.

In his introduction to *Dusk*, Philip Gourevitch has a great line: "He made language spare and lush all at once." When I first read this I thought, How can writing be both spare and lush? But Salter's somehow is. That's part of the mystery of how his sentences work. You could also say he is generous and harsh.

In a *Paris Review* interview, Salter says of maybe my favorite of his books, *Light Years:* "The book is the worn stones of conjugal life. All that is beautiful, all that is plain, everything that nourishes or causes to wither. It goes on for years, decades, and in the end seems to have passed like things glimpsed from the train—a meadow here, a stand of trees, houses with lit windows in the dusk, darkened towns, stations flashing by—everything that is not written down disappears except for certain imperishable moments, people and scenes. The animals die, the house is sold, the children are grown, even the couple itself has vanished, and yet there is this poem."

I say, "Most people don't think of their marriage that way. As things glimpsed from the train."

He says, "No, they are too involved. They're too warmly in it to think that way. I have a certain amount of detachment. I am observing."

It's the detachment in his work (the sliver of ice in his heart?) that made me think we could have this conversation; it's why I think he can help me. He is able to take the long view.

———

We are talking about work. The peculiar energy it bestows on the last years. I mention Sontag's determination to take any treatment without regard for suffering, to fight the disease to the end, to milk as much life as she could.

"That sounds like Peter Matthiessen," Salter says. "He wanted to have more time to write, no matter what." Matthiessen was one of his very old friends, a novelist, former editor of *The Paris Review*, former CIA agent in Paris, explorer, environmentalist, Buddhist. At eighty-six, Matthiessen fought his leukemia with grueling experimental drugs. He wanted to finish his last book, *In Paradise*. Salter didn't see him in the last weeks, but he heard that the treatment was harrowing.

I tell Salter the story of Tony Kushner thinking in the middle of a despairing phone call that Sendak might kill himself because he couldn't work and then driving all the way up to his house in Connecticut, only to find him stooped over his desk, covering the one eye that had been affected by cataract surgery, and working happily on his *Nose Book*. He'd figured out a way to work, and the crisis passed. As long as he could work, he could continue.

"That reminds me of Jules Feiffer," Salter says. "We just had dinner with him." The famous cartoonist, at eighty-six, is joyfully working in a new medium, the graphic novel. According to Salter, he is full of enthusiasm because he is still inventing, still drawing. He began a new form and is alive in it.

I say, "Updike wrote his last poems as he was dying." "Updike."
Salter pauses. "He wrote through anything." There may be
some old rivalry, some wryness in this comment: He says "Updike" with the tone of someone looking up at a darkening sky
and saying, "Rain."

He's not uninterested, though. I tell him about Updike writing
with his last bit of energy. How he put his head down on his
typewriter when he got home from the hospital and said, "I
can't do it," but then forced himself to type. How he took his
magnificent work ethic to his hospital bed, how it saved him, or
maybe "saved" is too romantic an idea here. How it organized
that last stretch, elevated those painful days, how it bestowed
on that bitter time some purpose, until it didn't anymore. How
he wrote to his editor: "The Endpoint theme came crashing
home, and so have pushed myself to take this as far as I can."

"I will always be writing something," Salter says. "But probably won't be something as glorified as a poem or a novel." He
pauses. "I will be writing a letter." I look at him. "That's not a
promise." He looks out the screen window at the trees.

———

When Salter was fifty-five, his twenty-five-year-old daughter,
Allan, died in an electrical accident. She was in the shower in a
cabin next door to his in Aspen. He walked in and found her
lying naked on the floor, the water running. He carried her
dead body in his arms. He took her outside and tried to resus-

citate her, somehow thinking she was drowning. We do not talk about this.

He says only, "There was the wreckage of that."

He has never written more than a few lines about it. In his memoir, he writes instead about another daughter, Nina, who had an infection in France when she was eleven and how he dreamed that she died. He writes, "The death of kings can be recited but not of one's child." He musters this formality for a reason. He is marking out territory. There are things you don't have to write. There are things you don't have to talk about. There are things that you don't need to resolve into words.

I read a piece about Salter somewhere in which his wife, Kay Eldredge, said, "He thinks it's important not to reveal everything, in part so the mystery of things won't dissolve. I'm closer to him than anybody, and there are still great pockets of isolation and privateness." In his introduction to *Dusk*, Philip Gourevitch says it another way: "For everything that is described, even more is evoked."

Salter tells me he is reading Heidegger. He tells me what interests him most in Heidegger is the gap between the said and unsaid.

Heidegger also wrote about the importance of being aware of *das Nichts* (the nothing, death). He was asked once how we could better lead our lives and he said we should spend more time in graveyards.

One freezing winter day, my eleven-year-old saw the Harry Potter–ish gates of the Green-Wood Cemetery in Brooklyn from the car window. She said, "You know, it clears your head to run down a hill in a cemetery," so her father drove us through the eerie streets of the dead and stopped so she could get out. She took her five-year-old brother and they both trudged up to the top of the hill and ran, hair flying, barreling past graves, while we waited at the bottom in the car with the door open. They flew back in, red-cheeked, cold. "Did that clear your head?" I asked, and they both said, "Yes!"

I think of Updike waking up the day after his lung cancer diagnosis and asking Martha for a piece of scrap paper, and her taking the blue cover of *My Father's Tears* from her purse so he could write on the back, because that was the only paper she had; I think of Sendak telling Lynn that he didn't want to see his dog, Herman, in the hospital, that he was done with life; I think of David Rieff's deep and tortured commitment to his mother's ideas in extremis, and of her bravery and resolve in the face of pain; I think of Freud refusing painkillers so he could think clearly about what was happening to him, until he chose the precise moment of morphine-aided oblivion; I think of Dylan Thomas drinking eighteen—or however many— whiskeys as a detective stood watching him from a dark corner of the bar, so he didn't have to think clearly about what was happening to him.

In even the worst deaths, observed closely, there is a great burst of life. I don't want to be sentimental. I think of Sontag's epic fight against her cancer and am tempted to see something

271

heroic in it, something to admire in the fierceness and commitment, something inspiring. But I also think of David Rieff
writing, "To me, torture is not too strong or hyperbolic a
word."

The stories entangle: Both Sontag and Updike were reading
*The Death of Ivan Ilyich* in their last months; the younger
Updike had affairs to stave off his fear of mortality, and
Dylan Thomas in his last desperate days ran upstairs at a
party to sleep with the hostess while his mistress waited
downstairs.

SALTER: Most people want to die in their sleep.

ME: Yeah.

SALTER: A friend of mine said, "I wouldn't want that
   moment to pass unnoticed." I think he has something
   there.

ME: I don't know. Maybe.

SALTER: Maybe it's better *not* to die in your sleep.

ME: Freud had this idea of "heroic clarity." He wanted to
   be clearheaded and aware.

SALTER: It's very human to want to, you know, mark the
   moment.

ME: You're right. To be there and attentive.

SALTER: Something big is happening.

[He looks away.]

SALTER: I don't know what I'll do.

[I don't say anything.]

SALTER: Let's not talk too much about this.

Salter goes into the kitchen for more iced tea.

When he comes back, I say, "I am sorry to dredge up this depressing subject."

"This doesn't depress me!" he says. "It's not depressing."

Somehow we keep going back to the idea of being awake or alert for one's death, of marking the moment. "I am not sure it's true. It might be one of those things that sounds good," he says. "It's like Heidegger. The language is evasive yet strangely summoning."

Were there moments when he thought he would die? Once, in a flying exercise when he was a cadet, he lost his bearings in his plane. It was evening and the signal became weak. He was flying low and nearly out of fuel, with maps folded out in front of him. He remembered that there was a pamphlet, "What to Do If Lost," and he read it with a flashlight. He tried reciting *Invictus:* "I am the master of my fate . . ." He didn't want to pray, but finally he did say a few prayers. With the fuel running dangerously low, he saw what he thought was a park. He turned on his landing lights, which turned out to be a mistake, because he couldn't see, and he plowed into a tree. The plane lost a wing, and he could no longer control it. It careened up, its nose vertical, and the landing light flooded a house for a moment, then the plane crashed into the house. The family ran out—no one was hurt. He turned off the ignition. As he breathed, he felt like his teeth were loose. He stepped out of the plane onto what had been the porch of the house. That night, he lay on a feather bed in the home of the mayor of Great Barrington, Massachusetts. He was too jittery to sleep, replaying the scene over and over in his head. "Afterward I had nightmares," he tells me. "I couldn't erase it."

———

When the terror of death blows through you, what do you do? What do you reach for? Aside from, of course, a drink or another person. When Salter's daughter died, he recited the only psalm he could mostly remember. He said prayers the night his plane scraped into trees and crashed into a house. In his last days, Updike kept *The Book of Common Prayer* next to his bed and prayed with Martha and the reverend who visited him. Even Sontag, a passionate atheist, called Peter Perrone to pray with her one morning. Not that this prayer comforted her or that she believed it for a second—even his description of her request is suffused with a high-level skepticism and irony—but, still, even she seems to have said a prayer.

To me, religion has never been consoling. I can't get anything out of even the cadences of it. It feels like a foreign language. I sometimes find the reassurance I imagine other people getting from religion in passages of novels, in poems. The words transform, tame. The perspective shifts. The world alters a little, for a few moments, to make death bearable or almost bearable. Sometimes if I read bits of poems I feel stronger, shored up. Like Dylan Thomas: "That the closer I move / To death, one man through his sundered hulks, / The louder the sun blooms / And the tusked, ramshackling sea exults;" or Updike: "God save us from ever ending, though billions have. / The world is blanketed by foregone deaths, / small beads of ego, bright with appetite."

The year I was sick and in and out of the hospital, there was one poem in particular that comforted me: Yeats's "Sailing to Byzantium." Even though I was twelve, I strongly identified with his line "That is no country for old men." The young are in one another's arms, the poem said, but you. You are outside all of that.

An aged man is but a paltry thing,
A tattered coat upon a stick, unless
Soul clap its hands and sing, and louder sing.

I wrote what was probably an unnaturally impassioned English paper on the poem. I really saw myself as that aged man. This is when I was coughing up blood and telling doctors I was fine. Yeats seemed to be speaking directly to me:

Consume my heart away; sick with desire
And fastened to a dying animal
It knows not what it is; and gather me
Into the artifice of eternity.

"Fastened to a dying animal." That part I got. And then comes the implausible and weirdly uplifting part: There is a place called Byzantium, an eternal world of art, a place where words exist forever, out of time. The poem ends with a vision of being reborn as a golden bird, forged in an eternal fire, who lives in Byzantium and sings to lords and ladies of what is past and passing and to come. Why would that golden bird comfort me? I have no idea. The words did.

It was also during the year I was sick that I began to compulsively keep notebooks. I wrote everything down—every inane fight with a friend; my fears about my upcoming operation; later, nights in Sheep Meadow in Central Park, drinking lime wine coolers with my friends, and problems with boyfriends—in cheap sketchbooks, composition pads, leather books, on both sides of the page. I couldn't bear the idea of losing anything, forgetting it, not having every single thing that happened to me in a tangible form I could hold. Later, these notebooks would become a liability, as I carted dozens around from apartment to apartment; nearly every man I ever loved read them, and some form of chaos or upheaval ensued. When I was married, I kept them at a trustworthy friend's house for safekeeping. Later, I put them in a strangely elegant leather suitcase with a lock, a very low-level bargain-basement Byzantium, but there it is.

Salter puts it this way in *Burning the Days:* "Life passes into pages if it passes into anything."

——

Salter talks about going to see his very close friend Irwin Shaw in Switzerland, as Shaw was dying. By the time Salter arrived, Shaw was already dead. I remember what he wrote about this moment in *Burning the Days:* "I touched his hair, something I had never done in life. It was like my own, curly, gray. I wanted to remember everything and at the same time never to have seen it." This is how I feel now about the deaths in this book. "I wanted to remember everything and at the same time never to have seen it."

At times in our conversation, Salter seems to be saying to me: "Why would I be thinking about dying on this glorious August day? And, furthermore, if I, in my late eighties, am not thinking about dying, why are you, in your forties, with children still needing you to pour cereal, thinking about dying?" He is not in fact saying this; he is, among other things, too gentlemanly to say this, and more open to rueful lines of thought, but his stoicism, his toughness, raises the question anyway. Maybe I don't need to think about it. Maybe you take your knowledge and move on.

———

Why does it matter to me now? I am talking to the frightened girl in the blue satin nightgown in the hospital, a tray with orange Jell-O and one of those little half cans of ginger ale in front of her.

I am trying to tell her that these death stories are okay. They are not really okay, because in each case someone dies, and there may, in fact, be no less-okay thing than that. But it's okay for this reason: If you have to let go, you can. You can find or manufacture a way to.

————

The fear returns, or it never goes away. It remains in the form of some fierceness I know springs from those weeks in the hospital. I would not be who I am without the fear.

When I have my first baby, I go back to the hospital. The baby is one month early. The surgeon does an emergency cesarean, because I am losing amniotic fluid. The baby is four pounds but she is breathing on her own. Earlier that day, when it became clear that something was going very wrong, I had asked the sonogram technician if she could just tell me if the baby was dead or alive. She said I would have to wait and speak to the doctor, and so I waited in the hallway on a bench for the doctor for forty minutes without knowing if the baby was dead or alive.

Hours later, in the operating theater, the blue scrubs, the paper on the gurney, the face masks, arouse something in me. I begin to panic; my heart races; my blood pressure rises dangerously. I try to picture an empty beach with palm trees, but the hospital intrudes.

For days after the cesarean, my heart rate stays dangerously elevated. The doctors can find nothing wrong with me, no preeclampsia, no pregnancy complication, but I can't stop panicking. The hospital—even the happy maternity ward, with its babies wheeled in glass prams, its new mothers, shocked and queenly, shuffling their way through the halls in robes—is making me panic; any doctor who comes near me with a stethoscope around her neck makes me panic; the mysterious, undetectable thing wrong with me, which ironically is panic, makes me panic. At night, I have trouble breathing.

When the nurses measure my blood pressure, they measure it again, because they think they must have gotten it wrong. The doctors put me on a magnesium drip to slow my heart. It feels like a truck is running through my brain. The room is blurred. My thoughts are gluey, slowed. There is a chair next to my bed, where my husband should be, but he is in the office. Even though we will not separate for two and a half years, it is now that he leaves. I hold my skinny baby. I am thinking that we will die.

———

Salter tells me about one of his commanders, Colonel Brischetto, very confident, very little flying experience. They were all going to North Africa to a gunnery camp, and they were waiting on the runway. The airplanes flew off in pairs. The colonel was flying with a wingman. He made a request to change radio channels, but he did not pull the lever correctly on the indicator and lost communication with the other plane. He had turned too sharply to the left and then corrected, and then he had lost his bearings in the clouds. Salter says it's easier than you'd think in the sky to lose the sense of where the earth is. The colonel turned downward.

"Cousin Echo," the wingman called. "I've lost you." The wingman couldn't follow and broke off and flew away. He tried the colonel on the radio several times but got no response. Salter imagines the colonel looking down at the channel selector for a few minutes, since he didn't hear the radio, and losing track of where he was. For a second, Salter imagines, he saw the ground through the windshield. Salter writes, "If, even for a moment, he thought of bailing out, it was already too late. As if in a nightmare, in the final second his eyes smashed through surfaces." Salter and the other pilots on the ground knew something was wrong, because they heard an announcement that the runway was closed.

The colonel is hurtling through the clouds at full speed toward the ground. I am transfixed by this story. Once he gets below the clouds, he can see. He sees through the windshield of the plane, and for a split second he processes it, but how? "First there is the surprise of it," Salter says to me. "His mind has gone through a dimension. There in the soup."

Is there a moment of panic, or is it possible to let go, to give in, to go under? There in the soup. ("The soup" is pilot slang for being lost in the clouds when you can't see and are operating on instruments.)

Salter thinks he had seconds to be afraid.

———

ME: My father's death was very close to dying in his
   sleep.
SALTER: It was?
ME: Well, he had a heart attack and collapsed on the
   floor of the lobby of the building. My mother asked
   him if she should call an ambulance, and he said no.
   It was so quick, he didn't know it was happening to
   him.
SALTER: I don't know about that.
ME: What do you mean?
SALTER: Well, he probably felt pain.

This shocks me. That he would have been in pain. That he
would have time to think about what was happening to him. I
am not sure why I hadn't thought of him either feeling pain or
knowing in those minutes what was happening or having time
to wonder what was happening or to be afraid.

SALTER: He was probably thinking, Is this something that
   will pass?
ME: Maybe that's why he said no to calling an ambulance.
SALTER: Probably he was thinking about whether it would
   go away on its own. He was thinking, What's
   happening and will it go away? Or is this the end?

Did he panic? I am not able to let myself think of him panicking. Panic is not a feeling I can associate with my father, who,
like Salter, did not show weakness generally and fear specifically.

ME: You're probably right. I have told the story so many
   times. My father died suddenly. He didn't know what
   was happening to him. But it's wrong.
SALTER: Don't dwell on it.
ME: I guess in my head I whitewashed it, made it easier.
SALTER: Don't think about it.

Why had I never thought of pain? I had always thought of my
father's heart attack as so sudden he would feel nothing; I
thought that it was over in a second. But he spoke after he collapsed, so it was clearly not, in fact, over in a second. Why had
no one ever pointed that out to me before when I told the
story? Probably because this is not something someone would
say in normal civilized conversation. But this is not normal
civilized conversation, or it's the outer edges. This is where
this book has brought me.

Later, I look up heart attacks in *How We Die*. Sherwin Nuland
writes about the pain that most often accompanies heart attacks:
"It has been most commonly described by its sufferers as con-
stricting, or viselike. Sometimes it manifests itself as a crushing
pressure, like an intolerable blunt weight forcing itself against
the front of the chest and radiating down the left arm or up into
the neck and jaw. The sensation is frightening . . . because . . . it
is accompanied by awareness of the possibility (and quite a realistic awareness it is) of impending death."

Don't dwell on it. Don't think about it.

———

What is most devastating is the image of my father being afraid on the floor of his lobby. The idea that he didn't have time to be afraid had consoled me.

I am coming to see that the real thing I am afraid of is not death itself but the fear of death. This fear is not abstract to me. The knowing you are about to die. The panic of its approach. That is what seems unbearable to me. That's what I've been trying to write my way through.

But here's what I learned from the deaths in this book: You work. You don't work. You resist. You don't resist. You exert the consummate control. You surrender. You deny. You accept. You pray. You don't pray. You read. You work. You take as many painkillers as you can. You refuse painkillers. You rage against death. You run headlong toward it.

In the end the deaths are the same. They all die. The world releases them.

There is a photograph Annie Leibovitz took of Sontag after she was dead, in the Frank Campbell funeral home; it is like a triptych, with three different photos that look almost stitched together. With a gentle light coming from below, her cropped white hair smoothed back, Sontag is lying on a table in an elegant pleated dress from Milan, wrists bruised, hands folded over her stomach, as if she had died serenely.

I know this tranquillity is highly constructed—the lighting, the careful labor of the funeral home, the dress from a designer that

Sontag loved, the necklace draped around her neck, the stirring, wishful vision of the photographer—but it's still tranquillity. The struggle, once it's over, doesn't exist. The fight is calmed.

I have this idea that I can work through the problem of death, the way Sendak did in drawing after drawing, and be less afraid, but maybe you are never less afraid; you are just better able to get along with the fear.

Maybe the whole idea that I need to find a way to be less afraid is wrong. Maybe even the fear is tolerable. Maybe Salter's friend's idea of "marking the moment" involves diving into that fear. Maybe that fear is not impossible. Maybe you get through the terror because you have to get through the terror. For some reason I have unconsciously been thinking of death as something you let happen, as a partnership, an agreement you enter or wrangle your way into, which is wrong.

In the actual moment, you do not have a choice. Grace finds you. Acceptance hunts you down.

———

"The deaths kind of reassured me," I say. "It's hard to explain why."

"Try," Salter says.

It is hard to put this into words. I think of the letter Sendak wrote about visiting the old family friend who is dying. He is terrified of this visit. He can hardly bear the idea of it. But when he finally goes to see her, he writes about how strangely great it was. He writes that it was like gazing into something you've always been terrified of and finding it magnificent.

The beauty I found in these deaths was what surprised me, the life rushing in, the vastness of the work, the great, sometimes deranged seeming courage, the mad love in the last moments. I think of Updike's first wife, Mary, holding on to his feet in her last visit to him; of Caitlin hugging Thomas in his hospital bed, until the nurse pulled her off him; of Annie Leibovitz climbing into Sontag's hospital bed. Part of the creative work these people did, their art, was their lives themselves. There is something glorious in the conflagration of everything at the end. The beauty was what ambushed me.

I tell Salter about the snow-painting dream Sendak has in the hospital. How he sees Lynn lying on a divan in front of a giant backdrop of a Dickensian Christmas scene of a snowy town, with horse-drawn carriages. How he hated Christmas, and he hated snow, how he, in fact, had always called snow "white death," but somehow the dream was radiant. How even after he couldn't hold a brush or pen, he dreamed in paintings, his mind still producing art. How, through the sheer crazy force of his imagination, he transformed the terror and rage (snow, Christmas, white death) into something beautiful and consoling.

Salter likes this story as much as I do. He says, "We make our own comfort."

It's almost evening now. There is a chill in the air. The light tossed through the leaves is very much Salter's light, an extravagant dark gold. I think of what he said: "The language is evasive yet strangely summoning."

I do not have a car and do not know how to drive. I have been planning to walk from Salter's house into town. He doesn't like this plan. He says he'll drive me. When we stand up I notice he is wearing sandals with socks. He reminds me suddenly of my father, who never wore sandals and socks. He drives me to the main street. We chat about his going off in a week to the University of Virginia, where he will teach a fiction seminar and give a series of talks.

"Send me the book!" he calls out the half-open window.

———

And I meant to send it to him. After I finished, I thought I would wait until I had made a few more changes, until it was in the form I wanted him to see. Months drifted by, and when I thought of sending it to him, I decided I still might make a few more little changes, and it wasn't quite good enough for him to see. Then, in June, I got a phone call saying that he had died. I was sitting on a deck in East Hampton, a tangle of trumpet flowers in a cerulean pot, late afternoon sun silver in the bay, and felt dizzy.

It had not occurred to me that he might die. I had thought of him teaching at the University of Virginia, pictured how the students would love his gruffness, would struggle for even the most minor or understated praise. I thought while on the phone, This can't be right.

He had a heart attack in the gym, a few days after his ninetieth birthday party. He celebrated it at Peter Matthiessen's widow's house in Sag Harbor, with a couple dozen of his friends. He had worn a white linen suit.

———

I thought of his evocation of the heart attack, his entering into it. I saw how steadily he could look, how much fortitude he could have in looking away. I thought of the colonel flying toward the earth in the soup, the place you navigate without instruments. I thought of how he said, "We make our own comfort." Those were the words I was looking for but couldn't get to: We make our own comfort.

# Acknowledgments

My biggest debt is to the people who spoke to me for this book. Many of them were revisiting a very arduous time, and I am hugely grateful to them for their generosity and trust in sharing their observations. I learned a lot from all of them.

Thanks to David Rieff for several conversations in which he helped and dazzled me enormously with his erudition and insight while adroitly answering exactly none of my questions; to Sharon DeLano for many lunches, her invaluable guidance and interpretations, her editorial advice, and her faith in me; to Stephen Koch for his memories and analysis; to Sookhee Chinkhan for her perspective; to Anne Jump for her recollections and corrections; to Peter Perrone for marathon conversations in his East Village walk-up and for his openness and point of view; to the night nurses for sharing their perspective on Sontag's last nights; to Martha Updike, who so graciously and intelligently and openly narrated Updike's last two months—without her that chapter would be a pale shadow of itself; to Mary Weatherall, Updike's first wife, for her graceful, honest reminiscences, for her admirable clarity; to Miranda Updike and Elizabeth Cobblah for their stories about that last few weeks; to David Updike for a conversation I'll always remember and for all of his help; to Michael Updike for his singular, funny sensibility and for sharing his understanding; to Dick Purinton for describing his last afternoon with Updike, for his wonderful photograph, and for the golf descriptions; to Lynn Caponera for her hospitality and great generosity with her memories and theories—without her I would not have nearly as rich a sense of my subject; and to Jonathan Weinberg for all of our in-depth conversations, for his ideas about art, his patient tutorials, his guidance through the Metropolitan Museum of Art, and his insights into Sendak and reflections on biography and subjectivity; to Tony Kushner for his gorgeous writing on Sendak and for his candid conversation and analysis; to Hilma Wolitzer for digging up high school memories.

I am also indebted to the libraries and special collections that house the archives I used: Houghton Library at Harvard, and Leslie Morris for helping me navigate the collection; the New York Psychoanalytic Institute; the Rosenbach Museum and Library; the Harry Ransom Center at the University of Texas, Austin; the Sigmund Freud Archives, Inc.; the Freud Museum, London, and the Library of Congress; and the Charles E. Young Research Library's Department of Special Collections at UCLA. I am also grateful to the various estates for their kind permission to quote from crucial texts and for their sometimes arduous consideration of my sometimes pushy requests.

Huge thanks to my beloved and patient editors, Susan Kamil and Noah Eaker, and to my amazing agent and old friend, Suzanne Gluck. Thanks also to Amelia Zalcman, who maybe heard a little too much from me. I've been incredibly lucky in my research assistants, Laura Smith and Maddie Gressel, who, along with their extraordinary work, also make everything more fun. Thanks also to Andrew Keese for his research assistance from afar. I am indebted to Adam Begley for talking me through arcane Updike issues and for his generosity with his scholarship. Thanks also to Dean Richard Kalb at New York University for the opportunity to try out one of these chapters as a lecture to excellent undergraduates in the scholars' lecture series.

I am grateful to my mother, Anne Roiphe, for support of this project, which went far beyond her contractual obligations as my mother. Thanks, also, for everything from talking through issues and ambivalences, to reading drafts, to general encouragement of this crazy project: Harry Chernoff, Theodore Jacobs, Radha Ramkissoon, Janet Malcolm, Amanda Brainerd, Casey Greenfield, Deborah Copaken, Hanna Rosin, Meghan O'Rourke, Judith Thurman, Jean Roiphe, Emily Roiphe, Daniel Swift, Caroline Moorehead, Larissa MacFarquhar, Leo Roiphe, and Violet Chernoff, and to Tim Nye, my late-arriving inspiration, salvation, etc.

# Notes on Sources

The title *The Violet Hour* comes from T. S. Eliot's *The Waste Land*. To me, the phrase evokes the mood of the elusive period I am describing: melancholy, expectant, laden. It captures the beauty and intensity I was finding in these scenes, the rich excitement of dusk. It is a poem obsessed with the nearness of death in many registers, irreverent, manic, and elegiac. Its famous line brings to mind the work all these writers did: "These fragments I have shored against my ruins."

## SUSAN SONTAG

This book first came into focus when I was working on a review of David Rieff's fascinating and tortured account of his mother's death, *Swimming in a Sea of Death*. Sontag's extraordinary response to her final illness made me think of exploring other writers' approaches to mortality and delving more deeply into hers.

I began researching this chapter using her notebooks and manuscripts, most of which I read for the first time in the Sontag archive at UCLA. I also spent some time immersed in the letters in the Farrar, Straus & Giroux collection in the New York Public Library.

My work in the archives quickly led to the inescapable and, to me, semi-alarming idea that I would have to talk to live people. I had lunch with David Rieff, who managed to be completely reticent yet hugely helpful. I met with Sharon DeLano in her Chelsea apartment. At first, her demeanor was daunting and a little gruff, and I thought she would decide she did not want to talk to me. But over a long period of time, she filled in an enormous amount of background on Sontag's last weeks for me. Sharon also gave me her email correspondence from that period, which was a hugely valuable resource, as was a calendar from Annie Leibovitz's office that helped me sort out the logistics of that time. In conversation, Sharon is sharp, funny, and insightful. I could see that she would be a superb editor. Mysteriously, she seemed almost to have played an editor's role in some of her friends' lives, advising them, tinkering with their problems, and straightening things out.

I met with Peter Perrone in his incense-scented East Village walk-up, and we talked for hours about his time with Susan as her caretaker, when he sometimes spent as much as sixteen hours a day with her. I also talked to Sookhee Chinkhan and two of the night nurses who were hired to be with Susan at the end. In addition, I talked to Anne Jump, Susan's last assistant, and Stephen Koch, her old friend.

I talked to Annie Leibovitz only once, and briefly. I was accidentally seated next to her at a book fair at my old school, Brearley, on the Upper East Side. I introduced myself and mentioned that I was working on this book, and she told me that Susan's bravery at the end was "too much." This seemed to be something that everyone I talked to subsequently agreed upon, even if they agreed on little else. Her bravery was too much. I tried to arrange a more formal conversation later, but Annie had by then decided not to talk to me. I pored over her photographs, combed through her introductions and interviews, to piece together some of her thinking on the subject, but it is mostly other people's accounts of her actions that inform the book.

All of Sontag's work fed into this chapter, but most central to my thinking were *Illness as Metaphor, Regarding the Pain of Others* (I often thought of that title in the years I spent basically regarding the pain of others), *On Photography*, the stories in *I, Etcetera, Death Kit*, and "The Way We Live Now," along with her play about Alice James, *Alice in Bed*.

## SIGMUND FREUD

Freud was a major part of my Ph.D. dissertation, "The Writer and the Dream," and coming from a family of psychoanalysts, I feel that I have been absorbing his atmosphere my whole life. I originally became interested in his death because of the enviable control he seemed to wield at the end, and because of his complex and resonant writing on mortality.

In thinking about my father's smoking, I became interested in Freud's smoking: Why did he, otherwise a good patient, a rational scientist, continue to smoke against the advice of his physicians? I began work on this chapter by combing through his letters and other people's observations for clues. Freud's own letters helped me unpack his relation to smoking, as well as his personal physician Dr. Max Schur's account of the conversations they both did and didn't have on the subject.

Absolutely vital to this chapter was Peter Gay's superb biography, *Freud: A Life for Our Time,* along with the three volumes of Ernest Jones's biography, *The Life and Work of Sigmund Freud.* I also found extremely fascinating Mark Edmundson's *The Death of Sigmund Freud,* which has an intriguing analysis of Freud's thinking and how it dovetailed with the rise of fascism. For insight into Anna Freud, I turned to Elisabeth Young-Bruehl's *Anna Freud: A Biography,* and for background on Marie Bonaparte, *Marie Bonaparte: A Life,* by Célia Bertin. Much of the medical information, in addition to many details of Freud's relationship to sickness and of his final months, comes from Max Schur's vivid account, *Freud: Living and Dying.*

Freud's letters were the richest source for this chapter: *Letters of Sigmund Freud,* edited by Ernst L. Freud; *The Complete Correspondence of Sigmund Freud and Karl Abraham, 1907–1925,* edited by Ernst Falzeder; *Sigmund Freud and Lou Andreas-Salomé, Letters,* edited by Ernst Pfeiffer; *The Complete Letters of Sigmund Freud to Wilhelm Fliess, 1887–1904,* edited by Jeffrey Moussaieff Masson, along with several other collections.

The works of Freud's I drew most directly on for this book are "Beyond the Pleasure Principle," "Thoughts for the Times on War and Death," *The Interpretation of Dreams,* and *Topsy: The Story of a Golden-Haired Chow,* by Marie Bonaparte, which Freud translated from French into German.

For a sense of Freud's house in Vienna, I relied on *Berggasse 19: Sigmund Freud's Home and Offices, Vienna 1938.* The Freud Museum, in London, has also been a very valuable resource for both information and a sense of place.

In addition, several very intriguing letters and telegraphs from the Anna Freud archive at the Library of Congress made their way into the book. Anna Freud's exchanges with Dorothy Burlingham in particular give a more intimate glimpse of her father's final days.

## JOHN UPDIKE

Many of the details I have of the last weeks of Updike's life come from his second wife, Martha Updike, who was generous enough to describe them to me over the course of several very long phone calls. I felt in these conversations both her enormous charm and the daunting strength of character other people described. I felt a strong urge to please her that I didn't quite understand.

Many of the scenes I describe were gleaned from interviews with the Updike children. David biked to meet me in Harvard Square, and we talked for three hours. Michael, who carves gravestones, among other things, and I had a couple of sprawling phone conversations, and I emailed with Elizabeth and Miranda. Someone said to me, "Martha's children were always more likely to be stockbrokers; Updike's children were more likely to be artistic types." His children were unfailingly open about the difficulties of Updike's last months—and life with him generally—as well as the exhilarations of both. Mary, his first wife, was also kind and open in giving her perspective. I was very struck by how fair and affectionate she seemed, how little she expressed of the bitterness divorced people usually harbor, how simply and clearly she was able to narrate both the spectacular and the arduous sides of life with a man like Updike.

I also found my conversation with Dick Purinton, Updike's old friend and golf buddy, extremely helpful. In our conversation, I understood as much about what they didn't talk about over the years as what they did. I grasped, for the first time, the liberation Updike must have felt when he ambled through lush Irish golf courses with his friends.

Much of my sense of his illness, and his dedication to work, came from a trip to the Updike archives at Harvard's Houghton Library. The handwritten manuscripts of the final poems were particularly startling, as the handwriting itself told a story about the sheer effort it took to get the words on the page. One can know this abstractly, or have it described, but it is very different to see it in the spidery letters themselves, the slanted lines, the scratched-out words.

Updike's correspondence is so charming and lively and wonderful that it evokes the man more powerfully than his published bits of autobiography; I also got a more tangible sense of how many of his relationships existed mostly in writing. He had close friends, like Warner Berthoff, who lived and taught at Harvard but whom he rarely saw, though they exchanged intimate letters for decades. One also saw how connected he was to many famous literary figures, though he deliberately lived outside the literary hub of New York City. The isolation was physical, but his letters were sociable, chatty, engaged. It may not be surprising that much of the work of friendship, for Updike, existed on the page.

Adam Begley's wonderful biography, *Updike*, was a tremendous resource for this chapter. He also talked me through some of the issues that were bewildering me, such as Updike's religious commitment. I was flummoxed by Updike's irony, specifically by how he could be so ironic about religion but serious about it as well, and Begley talked me through that particular apparent contradiction. He was generous with his impressions and observations, and my talking things through with him helped sharpen the narrative.

All of Updike's novels and stories, along with his autobiography, *Self-*

*Consciousness,* were rich sources for this chapter, as were his interview with *The Paris Review* and many of his articles. Updike took all of his pieces so seriously and unhackishly that it's awe inspiring. I once read a piece he wrote for *Allure* on sunscreen that was such a beautiful and tiny lyrical masterpiece that it put the rest of us journalists and writers to shame. It was, of course, the poems collected in *Endpoint* that first startled and obsessed me when they appeared in *The New Yorker* and made me think of Updike for this book—along with my love of his work and my special interest in his linking of adultery and immortality. I have a soft spot for those who try to defeat death with sex.

## Dylan Thomas

Dylan Thomas's letters are charming, maddening, gorgeous, and perhaps the inspiration for much of my story of his final weeks. He was, of course, brilliant at diagnosing himself, putting his spectacular malaise into words. Who but he could come up with the sublime phrase "self-destroyed escapologist"? The books of letters that were most helpful were: *The Love Letters of Dylan Thomas*, by Dylan Thomas; *Selected Letters of Dylan Thomas*, by Constantine Fitzgibbon; *Dylan Thomas: Letters to Vernon Watkins*, by Dylan Thomas; *A Pearl of Great Price: The Love Letters of Dylan Thomas to Pearl Kazin*, edited by Jeff Towns.

For the cloud of controversy surrounding his last days, along with some of the detail, I found the letters and documents at the Harry Ransom Humanities Research Center in Texas to be a huge resource. What struck me most about the firsthand accounts of Thomas's conversations was the analytical brio evidenced there, the atmosphere of paranoia, rife with richly detailed accusations and passions ruffled and roused. Many of his friends seemed to write about his death as if they were being deposed by lawyers, or building a case. No one was claiming he was murdered, of course, but there was a *feeling* akin to that for them. Then there were other intriguing minutiae: the autopsy report, letters from his bank in England, doctor's opinions. For the texture of those last days before he went into a coma, those documents were invaluable. I was particularly enthralled by the notebook kept by the detective following him around for his last days, as he is a kind of shadow stand-in for any biographer.

For biographical background, I am indebted to *Dylan Thomas: The Biography*, by Paul Ferris and *The World of Dylan Thomas*, by Peter Stevenson. I also found very useful Dr. William Murphy's "Creation and Destruction: Notes on Dylan Thomas." Another great resource for background into Thomas's life was a series of curated interviews collected in *Dylan Remem-*

*bered*, both volumes edited by David N. Thomas. In order to understand more clearly some of the conspiracy thinking that sprung up around his death, I read *The Death of Dylan Thomas*, by Dr. James Nashold and George Tremlett.

Thomas's poems were, of course, the most important of his works analyzed here, but, additionally, *Under Milk Wood, A Child's Christmas in Wales, Portrait of the Artist as a Young Dog*, and *Dylan Thomas: The Collected Stories* all fed into this chapter.

Listening to Thomas reading his poems was one of the more fruitful things I did for this chapter. The cadences of his voice summoned him in ways I couldn't have anticipated, and suggested interpretations of the poems that I couldn't have come to by reading the words on the page. In seventh grade, I won a poetry recitation contest at school with "Do Not Go Gentle into That Good Night," and his spoken version greatly challenged my ancient understanding of that poem.

I found the memoirs of those who knew him enormously useful in providing a kaleidoscopic impression of the complicated man, especially his daughter Aeronwy Thomas's memoir, *My Father's Places*, and Caitlin Thomas's spirited memoir, *Leftover Life to Kill*. John Malcolm Brinnin's *Dylan Thomas in America: An Intimate Journal* is a great book to read especially to apprehend the fanatical adoration that shadowed Thomas on his late trips to America. I especially love Elizabeth Hardwick's essay on Thomas's death, collected in *A View of My Own*, for its analysis of the American reaction and the role it played. The poets who remembered him, John Berryman, Robert Lowell, and Elizabeth Bishop, were also wonderful in capturing the man in a few choice words. He was blessed with very talented onlookers.

## MAURICE SENDAK

Like nearly everyone under fifty, I came to Maurice Sendak as a child, his books glimmering in my unconscious landscape, the images deeply, sleepily familiar. When he died, I read an interview that mentioned him saying he wanted a "yummy death" like William Blake's, which immediately drew me in. After a little digging, I became fascinated by his attitude toward death, the irreverence, the deep obsessive engagement; he seemed to me a fellow traveler.

The books of his that resonate most deeply in this chapter are *Where the Wild Things Are, In the Night Kitchen, Bumble-Ardy, Higglety Pigglety Pop!, Outside Over There*, and the strange and lovely *My Brother's Book*. I imposed *Outside Over There* on my then-four-year-old son more than once, only to hear that it was "too scary." "Good scary, though" I tried, though that was not a concept he was willing to entertain. The scariness, anyway, is eloquent, communicating a bone-deep loneliness, fears most people are not willing to give voice to, to unloose.

I actually found it a transcendently great experience to return to the books as an adult, reading on my own and not to children, who, let's face it, can be a distraction from truly taking the stories in: Their meanings are different when you have the luxury of living with them; the communication occurs on a whole other level. I also found Sendak's essays on children's literature, *Caldecott & Co.*, particularly illuminating in terms of his thinking about the craft.

Most of the rich background of his life that infuses this chapter came from people very close to him who very generously gave me their time, opened their doors, made me lunch, and shared their memories. The art historian Jonathan Weinberg invited me to his incredible portrait-strewn New Haven house, where we climbed upstairs to his studio so I could ask him questions while he painted a portrait of me. Our conversations were ongoing, about Maurice, about Eugene Glynn, whom Jonathan loved, about art. He talked me through Sendak's illustrations, his influences, et cetera, and he gave me a great deal of perspective on Sendak's world.

Tony Kushner talked to me about Sendak at a diner on the Upper West Side. His stories about Sendak, about their friendship, were critical in bringing across my impression of the man. For insight into his Bensonhurst days, his high school friend Hilma Wolitzer, who sat next to him in art class, recalled the teenage Sendak for me.

The afternoon I spent with Lynn Caponera, in which she made me sandwiches and we sat at the table where Sendak used to sit, was perhaps the richest source for the chapter. Most of what I wrote here springs from her view of the man, her observations, her descriptions. Her own story is fascinating—the decades-long relationship in which she was neither daughter nor mother nor housekeeper and instead was something transcending all of that. I couldn't help thinking that every writer and artist needs a Lynn, and almost none will ever find her. She seemed the perfect protector, muse, helper, friend. One of the things this book taught me is how fluid the boundaries of friendship can be, how extraordinary the roles are that people fall into with each other in unusual and creative forms of love.

Sendak's vast number of remarkable radio, television, and print interviews—which are funny, wild, brilliant—were hugely helpful in creating this portrait, along with Tony Kushner's lovely reminiscence in *The Guardian*. In particular, the long interviews in *The Believer* and *The Comics Journal* were especially compelling, as were his late appearances on *Fresh Air with Terry Gross, The Colbert Report* with Stephen Colbert, and *NOW with Bill Moyers.* Tony Kushner's superb and gorgeously written *The Art of Maurice Sendak: 1980 to the Present,* was also enormously informative and insightful, as was Selma G. Lanes's earlier volume, *The Art of Maurice Sendak.*

Perhaps the most valuable resource for this chapter was the letters and manuscripts in the Sendak archive, which at the time was housed at Philadelphia's Rosenbach Museum and Library. His correspondence is extraordinary, and reveals him to be as much a writer as an artist. His letters also convey a generous side, a great warmth toward others, that does not necessarily come through in his carefully curated public persona. He is, in the correspondence, funny, charming, whimsical, and a great warmhearted friend to a large number of people. Bountifully evident throughout is his gift for intimacy. I was particularly struck by his decades-long correspondence with Minnie Kane, who began as a fan and admirer and became, from afar, a close and cherished correspondent who sent him little stones as gifts. After some deliberation, the Sendak estate refused to give me permission to quote from these letters, believing Sendak's intention was to have all his letters destroyed, which was a great loss for this book and for Sendak scholarship in general.

Seeing the voluminous drafts of the manuscripts and drawings, the tiny dummy books, the preliminary sketches on vellum, was electrifying: the early text for *In the Night Kitchen,* scrawled on yellow legal paper, the recipe for cake written on orange paper—with shortening, eggs, sugar, orange flower water—the later versions, where the terrifying oven is toned down and then toned down further. The exhortations to himself in the margins to make things better and clearer. All this brought home the sheer amount of work that went into Sendak's art, the absolute devotion he had to it. I had heard from other people that he did more work than most illustrators, threw himself more deeply into the process, but this fact came alive to me when I saw the manuscripts. The evolution of the drawings and text allowed me to glimpse the arc of his imaginative process in a way that conjured the man as nothing else had.

I also spent a memorable afternoon at Sendak's wonderful house in Ridgefield, Connecticut, with Lynn Caponera, and it's there that I saw the manuscript of *The Nose Book,* which was then sitting on the desk in his studio. I felt lucky to see his environment up close: the Keats mask in its box in a guest bedroom with a blue bedspread, his collection of Mickey Mouses, his Blake drawing, Melville's portable writing desk, his ancient kitchen appliances. Most of my descriptions of the place spring from that visit.

## James Salter

I was drawn to the idea of talking to James Salter for this book without entirely understanding why. I return to his books, *Light Years*, *A Sport and a Pastime*, *Dusk and Other Stories*, and *All That Is*, over and over. They contain for me some mysterious perspective on life that I am compelled to go back to. I find them reassuring, beautiful; they complete some train of thought I wasn't entirely aware of having. So when I emailed Salter, out of the blue, asking him to talk about death with me, I was surprised and excited when he said he would. I realized it might be good to include in this book a writer I could talk to, that after years of circling my subjects, reading their journals and letters, tracking down their friends and families, it might be useful to talk to a writer himself, one old enough to be facing death in some way, and one tough enough to talk about that confrontation. My conversation with Salter veered into territory I couldn't have predicted, and it was in talking to him that radiant afternoon in August that some of the restlessness of this book quieted down. I had the feeling, finally, of finding what I was looking for, or of suddenly being able to see the subject in a new way, a way I could live with. I'll always be grateful to Salter, for his generosity in having that conversation, for his kindness, for his inimitable way with words, and for his rare instinct about when not to use them.

301

# Photo Credits

Page 25: Susan Sontag's loft on Seventeenth Street in New York City. Photo by Dominique Nabokov.

Page 77: Sigmund Freud's study in Hampstead, London. Photo courtesy of Freud Museum London.

Page 111: John Updike's desk at his home in Beverly Farms, Massachusetts. Photo by Leslie A. Morris © 2009 President and Fellows of Harvard College.

Page 159: Dylan Thomas's writing shed in Laugharne, Wales. Photo courtesy of Aled Llywelyn/Alamy.

Page 201: Maurice Sendak's home studio in Ridgefield, Connecticut. Photo courtesy of Todd Heisler/The New York Times/Redux.

Page 289: James Salter's office in his home in Bridgehampton, New York, on June 19, 2015, the day of his death. Photo by Kay Eldredge.

# Permissions

## About the Author

KATIE ROIPHE is the author of several books, including *The Morning After: Sex, Fear, and Feminism; Uncommon Arrangements: Seven Marriages; In Praise of Messy Lives: Essays;* and a novel, *Still She Haunts Me.* Her essays and articles have appeared in *The New York Times, The Washington Post, The New Yorker, The Paris Review, The Wall Street Journal, Financial Times, Harper's, Vogue, Esquire, Slate,* and *Tin House.* She has a Ph.D. in literature from Princeton University and is the director of the Cultural Reporting and Criticism program at New York University. She lives in Brooklyn.

## About the Type

This book was set in a Monotype face called Bell. The Englishman John Bell (1745–1831) was responsible for the original cutting of this design. The vocations of Bell were many—bookseller, printer, publisher, typefounder, and journalist, among others. His types were considerably influenced by the delicacy and beauty of the French copperplate engravers. Monotype Bell might also be classified as a delicate and refined rendering of Scotch Roman.